No one said your twenties would be like this . . .

Cheap, spacious apartments, lazy afternoons spent caffeinating at the local coffee bar, financially rewarding jobs—life sure is fabulous when you're young, talented, ambitious, and . . . on *Friends*. But for those of us living in the real world, keeping one step ahead of the bills often becomes a full-time job in itself.

You *don't* need a lecture, you *won't* live a life of self-denial, you just want to get out of debt. *Debt-Free by 30* shows you how with a plan that is realistic, empathetic, and guaranteed effective. Written by two twentysomethings who've been there, this is an indispensable handbook for serious moneyphobes everywhere.

So relax, laugh a little, and let them clue you into getting a grip on your finances before you hit the big 3-0.

JASON ANTHONY is a film and television executive who has run the East Coast offices of some of the biggest producers and directors in Hollywood. He is also a freelance writer. He lives in New York City.

KARL CLUCK is a senior strategist at Razorfish, a leading Internet solutions agency. Previously he worked as a writer at Comedy Central where he co-produced *Mastercheese Theatre*, a weekly late-night tribute to the dumbest films in Hollywood. He lives in London.

debt-free
by **30**

Practical Advice for the

YOUNG, BROKE, &

UPWARDLY MOBILE

JASON ANTHONY
AND KARL CLUCK

A PLUME BOOK

PLUME
Published by the Penguin Group
Penguin Putnam Inc., 375 Hudson Street, New York, New York 10014, U.S.A.
Penguin Books Ltd, 27 Wrights Lane, London W8 5TZ, England
Penguin Books Australia Ltd, Ringwood, Victoria, Australia
Penguin Books Canada Ltd, 10 Alcorn Avenue, Toronto, Ontario, Canada M4V 3B2
Penguin Books (N.Z.) Ltd, 182–190 Wairau Road, Auckland 10, New Zealand

Penguin Books Ltd, Registered Offices: Harmondsworth, Middlesex, England

First published by Plume, a member of Penguin Putnam Inc.

First Printing, January 2001
10 9 8 7 6 5 4 3 2

 REGISTERED TRADEMARK—MARCA REGISTRADA

CIP data is available.
ISBN 0-452-28213-6

Printed in the United States of America

PUBLISHER'S NOTE
This publication is designed to provide accurate and authentic information in regard to the subject matter covered. It is sold with the understanding that the publisher is not engaged in rendering financial, accounting, or other professional service. If financial advice or other expert assistance is required, the service of a competent professional person should be sought.

*This book is dedicated to James and Venus Anthony
for three decades of love, faith, and support.
Some debts you can never repay.*

CONTENTS

ACKNOWLEDGMENTS

Whoever said writing is a lonely, solitary experience never had Tanya McKinnon for an agent. She's everything an agent should be: creative, collaborative, and responsive. Oh, and she works her ass off, too. The woman is a great agent and a better friend. We are privileged to have her in our corner.

Our editors at Plume, Jennifer Kasius and Amanda Patten, are members of that rare breed of editors who still actually edit. Editors oversee dozens of books a year, yet somehow each managed to make us feel we were their only writers. Their enthusiasm and suggestions made this a far better book.

Bill Eville and Stephen Shapiro are two very good friends who never shied away from telling us what worked and what sucked. This is especially impressive for Bill, because he worked for me at the time and I could have fired him. Amye Dyer helped us whip the proposal into shape.

I am especially grateful to Steven Anthony for patiently answering the questions of his mechanically hopeless son. Dad also hooked me up with Dominic Marsicovetere, a veteran C.P.A. and professor of Accounting at Hofstra University. Now I know everything I'll ever need to about death, taxes and Cher. Chris Clausen of the Clausen Agency was so helpful with the insurance chapter that I ended up buying my auto and renters policy from him.

For support both practical and emotional, we want to thank Mary Evans, Ravi Nandan, Elaine Chen, Stephanie Staal, Judi Farkas, Ray Parisi, Brian Jones, Jason Hallock, Stephanie Mueller, Stephen Larkin and of course, John, Peggye, and Hannah Cluck. Thank you, thank you, thank you.

To Will Speck, who despite his many "endearing" nicknames for me, actually believes in me more than I do (I think he does, anyway): I couldn't imagine my twenties—all right, forties—without him.

And finally, to all the twentysomethings who agreed to sit down with us and share their tales of financial woe: We told you you weren't alone.

INTRODUCTION

Jason and Karl Hit Rock Bottom

One Sunday a couple of years ago, I met my friend Karl for brunch. I was in a particularly foul mood that day. It was raining, the subway was late, and tomorrow was Monday, which meant another day at a film job that each day felt less like *The Player* and more like a cross between *Dilbert* and *Working Girl*. But while Dilbert only had to endure his boss four panels a day and Melanie Griffith eventually got her promotion, my own situation didn't promise a Hollywood happy ending. In my darkest moments, I imagined I was in the ninth circle of job hell and Satan sat in the corner office.

Karl asked me about a job offer I was considering. A friend had approached me about a position at her agency that would eventually lead to a partnership. It was a fantastic opportunity. Finally, I would be rescued from my present misery and be the entrepreneur I had always wanted to be. I would have to take a 15 percent pay cut for the first two years, but it seemed a small and temporary step back for such a terrific opportunity. When we had last spoken, I had told Karl I was close to accepting the offer. Now after some serious soul-searching, I told Karl I had to turn the offer down. He looked at me incredulously. Why?

The answer was almost too painful to admit: I was drowning in debt. That almost quaint freshman-year Visa card with the $500 credit limit felt like kid stuff now. Over the years that benign $500 had slowly ballooned to a $15,000 limit . . . and I was maxed out. After paying my bills each month—rent, credit cards, gym membership, student loans, utilities, etc.—I barely had enough for the subway. Though the pay cut would amount to less than $60 a week after taxes, even that small amount would send me teetering over the edge into the financial abyss. So even though I knew I was making a huge mistake, I turned the job down. I wasn't likely to get another chance at owning a stake of a business in an industry I loved, but I had no choice. Debt made the decision for me.

As brunch progressed Karl made some confessions of his own. Despite a comfortable salary and a good job, he too lived paycheck to paycheck. Sometimes he would run out of money midweek and take out cash advances just so he could eat. Faced with a steadily creeping credit card balance, he had shelved his plans for graduate school long ago because he couldn't afford the minimum credit card payments on a student's stipend. He told me of the time he read in the paper that the median annual income of the average American family was about $20,000 less than he earned. Even without the 2.2 kids and the mortgage, Karl was barely staying afloat.

Where did we go wrong? I hardly considered myself reckless or extravagant. I paid my bills on time, vacationed only where my frequent flier miles took me, and shopped at J.Crew and Banana Republic, hardly temples of *haute couture*. Judging from the number of credit card offers dumped in my mailbox each week, I assumed my credit rating must be in pretty good shape, too. I felt like a normal guy with a normal life. Yet all around me people my age were buying their first homes and having children and generally plowing full-steam ahead into prosperity. When my parents were my age, they had a house, their own business, and me. I was twenty-seven years old and my only "asset" was the security deposit on my apartment.

I pitched an idea to Karl. If we were so clueless and carefree with money on our own, maybe we should work together to get out of our individual messes. Karl looked at me and raised an eyebrow. "Like sponsors in those twelve-step programs?" he asked suspiciously. "No," I replied, "more like teammates. We could roll up our sleeves, do some work, and figure out what we're doing wrong. Think of it as reform school for debtors." It took a little more persuading, but after I convinced Karl that we wouldn't live like Benedictine monks, he agreed.

Then the real work began. Since our combined financial training consisted of a freshman-year economics class and the occasional *Forbes* magazine skimmed in the dentist's waiting room, we first turned to the experts. At the local bookstore we found books on family budgeting, saving for retirement, dying penniless (I probably didn't need to look at that one), and playing the market to win—in short, books that were of little use to the young and broke. We left frustrated and empty-handed.

Where was the book for us? We weren't looking for investment tips and we didn't need to be reminded that social security wouldn't be around to cushion us in our golden years. Even ordinarily good advice just didn't apply to our situation. For example, virtually every expert stressed over and over the importance of having a "safety net" equal to three months of total expenses. If we had that kind of self-discipline, we wouldn't be spending Saturday afternoon in the personal finance aisle.

For all the talk about our generation being the most independent and self-reliant, when it comes to handling money, most of us belong back in the womb. It's strange. We spend a good chunk of our first three decades in training for something, whether it's driver's ed, a foreign language, a career, the marathon, etc. But when it comes to financial planning, the vast majority of us are launched out to sea without so much as a life jacket. No wonder so many of us promptly sink. Even college, which supposedly prepares us for the real world, usually bypasses this critical part of adulthood. Yes, we go to school to broaden the mind (it's certainly the last time most of us will pick up *Ulysses*), but we also go for life training. Academia, with its inherent suspicion that money contaminates the intellectual soul, can actually discourage financial responsibility. Spend four years on a college campus and any impressionable young mind is bound to soak up some of those attitudes.

So is it any wonder so many of us become moneyphobic adults? Unprepared to deal with the reality that the free ride of childhood is officially over, we do what humans have done in the face of adversity for two thousand years. We go into denial. We pretend everything is the same as it ever was. We go on leading the life we grew accustomed to living, and we tell ourselves that somehow the bills will disappear the way they always have. The result: a charged-up, stressed-out twenties that can put a serious crimp in the future.

Karl and I realized that if we wanted to get out of debt we would have to take matters into our own hands. We first had to recognize our own moneyphobia. We had to acknowledge that money problems don't go away by pretending they don't exist. We had to accept the fact that nobody was going to bail us out of this mess, and that we had no one to blame but ourselves. Blaming our salaries, our rents, and the IRS wasn't going to get us out of debt. Most important, we couldn't be intimidated by the work we had ahead of us. Only then could we develop a course of action.

First, we sat down to figure out where the money was going. Every time we reached for our wallets we began to jot down what we were buying and why. We were stunned by what we learned. Karl found he was blowing over $1,000 a year on cabs, despite living in a city with a public transportation system second to none. I discovered that my coffee habit set me back a staggering $1,200 annually. (I prefer my caffeine dressed in a Frappuccino.) All those late video charges, ATM fees, and dry-cleaning deliveries nibbling away at both of our paychecks added up to one huge bite. It became very obvious that the cause of our financial woes wasn't the money we made, but how we spent it.

We became obsessed. We requested old checking statements (hopelessly disorganized), pored over old tax returns (including the pre-itemizing years), and took a microscope to our utility bills.

We spent more than a few Saturday afternoons in the library reading up on everything from credit card consolidators to the psychological roots of compulsive spending. We learned the best way to handle those early morning phone calls from American Express, as well as surprisingly legal ways to keep more of our money out of the greedy hands of the IRS. We saw how much money we were spending in pursuit of fun and looked for different, less costly ways to have a good time.

As we gradually let the air out of our debtload, it became clear to us that for too long we were on the losing side of our relationship to money. We no longer saw money as a root of anxiety, but as a means of self-determination. We stopped blaming money for keeping us from achieving our dreams and recognized that it held the key to financial and psychological liberation. The more we chipped away at our debt, the more self-confident and optimistic we became. Things were once again "possible." A huge weight had been lifted from our shoulders, a weight we had grown so used to carrying we forgot it was there.

Debt-Free by 30 is the happy result of our climb back to solvency. We understand from firsthand experience that money owed is only a fraction of the real price of debt. We know the diminished opportunities and emotional toll that come from living life in a financial straitjacket. Money strategies that look good on paper don't always work for a generation raised to expect a *Dynasty* lifestyle on a *Roseanne* budget.

This book won't ask you to clip coupons, buy weird brands of discount soda, or move back in with your parents. All it requires is a genuine commitment to changing your current financial situation so you can begin laying the foundation for the future rather than paying for the inexperience of the past. This book won't make you rich, but it will put you back in control of your money (and your life) sooner than you think. If two former financial basket cases with $27,000 of debt between them could do it, trust us—you can too.

debt-free
by **30**

1

The Seven Debtly Sins

If you're in your twenties and sinking in debt, you probably feel like your life has been put on hold. This was supposed to be your decade to conquer. You survived the rocky teenage years and the frat parties of college life. You're unencumbered by grown-up responsibilities like hefty mortgages and college saving plans for your kids. Your parents have stopped cracking the whip and finally treat you as an equal (more or less). You're a freshly minted adult, ready to take on the world.

But instead of a roaring twenties, you find yourself limping toward the big 3-0 one minimum payment at a time. At the rate you're going you fear you'll die in that fourth floor walk-up apartment. That brilliant small business idea you have will remain just that, because a good idea without capital is like a new car without gasoline—it gets you nowhere. And that short-term loan mom and dad generously floated you five years ago? Bad news: they haven't forgotten.

It's easy for us to make excuses for being in debt, especially people in their twenties just getting started. Many of us are still paying our dues professionally and working long hours for little pay. The days of overtime went out when your parents stopped driving you to work, and now all those Saturdays you spend in the office don't show up in your paycheck. If you're under twenty-five, you probably pay hundreds of dollars more every year for car insurance than a 31-year-old driving school dropout. You live paycheck to paycheck, and since most of your friends do too, you tell yourself you're powerless to do anything about it. Sure, you'll dig yourself out of the hole one of these years, but as each debt-laden New Year arrives that day fades farther and farther into the horizon.

HERE'S HOW YOU KNOW IF YOU NEED THIS BOOK

Before you can bail yourself out of debt, you need to identify the patterns and attitudes that got you there in the first place. With a pen, mark off those you are guilty of. Remember, no cheating! Confession may be good for the soul, but it's even better for your bank balance.

Are you a debtly sinner? Take this simple quiz and find out!

The Quiz

___ Do you max out your Visa now and hope your Christmas bonus will pay it off?

___ Do you immediately crumple up the ATM receipt to avoid looking at the balance?

___ Are you 28 years old and still asking your parents for cash on your birthday?

___ Do you sometimes pay costly medical bills rather than deal with frustrating insurance paperwork?

___ Have you ever prematurely sold an investment or prized possession to pay off some debts?

___ Do you agonize about how you will pay your debts if you suddenly lost your job?

___ Would you change to a more fulfilling but lower-paying job if you weren't in debt?

___ Have you ever rationalized buying something you didn't need because you were so hopelessly in debt that you thought, "What difference does a few more dollars make?"

___ Are friends in a similar income bracket beginning to pull ahead of you?

___ Do you regularly set deadlines for paying off your credit cards and then miss them?

___ Are you relying on a future inheritance to bail yourself out of your financial troubles?

___ Do you sometimes use one credit card to pay the monthly payment of another?

___ Have you ever taken a vacation you couldn't afford by promising yourself to pay it with next year's tax refund?

___ Do you frequently wonder why you have so little to show for all those years of work?

Now tabulate your score. Give yourself 1 point for every answer you checked off.

0 points: You win! You're well on the road to financial independence. Feel free to laugh at all your spendthrift friends when you retire at 35.

1–3 points: With a few minor lifestyle adjustments and a serious attack on your credit card balance, you should have no problem achieving your goal of debt-free living.

4–7 points: Unless you plan to give your firstborn to Sallie Mae (that's shorthand for Student Loan Marketing Association), you need to get serious about debt reduction and savings now. It might take a little self-discipline at first, but you'll thank us someday. We promise.

8–11 points: First the good news: Australia is no longer a penal colony for debtors. Now the bad news: At the rate you're going, you may have to hide halfway around the world to escape your creditors. Getting serious about changing your bad habits is the smartest thing you can do to for your future.

12–14 points: Oh my. Take a deep breath and relax. Help is on the way.

Regardless of your score, everyone can be smarter about managing money and staying out of debt. Here we explain some of the most common "sins" that send people in their twenties straight to debt hell.

Just remember, every one of you out there, regardless of whether you make $20,000, $50,000, or $100,000 a year, has the power to get out of debt. You must accept that you will always have far more control keeping the money you have than the amount of money you make. Don't wait for your first million before you shoot for solvency. Develop good habits now, and you will never have to worry about where the money will come from later.

Behold! Your route to redemption!

THE FIRST DEBTLY SIN:
THOU SHALT NOT COUNT ON FUTURE EARNINGS TO PAY PRESENT DEBT

Here's a cold splash of reality: it won't. For those of you who've been out in the work world awhile, think back to your first entry-level job and the accompanying pitiful salary. You probably look back and wonder, "How did I ever survive on that?" But you did, and you probably owed less money then, too. How does this happen?

For most of us, as we make more money we suddenly find we "need" more and more things to keep us happy. It's simply human nature to spend what we make. Spending rises with income, and, for twentysomethings, the appeal of more, shinier, newer stuff becomes difficult to resist. We all work hard for the life we want to lead, so it's understandably tempting to use a raise or promotion to crank our standard of living up a few notches instead of doing the responsible thing. After all, you can't wear a lower minimum payment. The cars get sportier, the apartments larger, and the designer labels more difficult to pronounce, and before you know it, you're sending your entire raise to Visa.

A bigger paycheck without a firm commitment to change your behavior guarantees only two things: bigger debt and more worry. I speak from experience. Thanks to a recent promotion, I more than doubled my salary from what I was making a few years ago. Now don't get me wrong; I wasn't about to crowd anyone out of the Fortune 500, but I was finally making an "adult" salary. I told myself my days of deficit spending were over. I had ambitious plans: I would pay off my credit cards, knock out my student loans, and begin squirreling away money for a down payment that would finally free me from the tentacles of my greedy landlord.

It didn't quite work out that way. Five nice suits and a couple of fancy vacations later, I had achieved the seemingly impossible: with twice the salary, I tripled my debt. The planned student loan KO softened to more of a slap: I was forced to defer, coming up with a story for the loan representative that would make Pinocchio proud. And, needless to say, I was still an indentured servant to my landlord.

In my case, getting a raise actually made my financial situation worse. The additional income burst the dam, and out flowed years of pent-up materialistic cravings. I had misjudged my newfound purchasing power, and what little self-restraint I once had flew out the window with my common sense. The world was mine! (If it took American Express.)

THE SECOND DEBTLY SIN:
THOU SHALT NOT BE A SLAVE
TO IMMEDIATE GRATIFICATION

Freud thought that the ability to delay pleasure is one sign of adulthood; the folks at Visa want you to believe instead that it takes a $10,000 credit limit before you can sit at the grown-ups' table. The rush that comes when we plunk down the plastic for the perfect shoes or the latest cell phone can be intoxicating, but when those bills start to pile up unpaid on the kitchen counter . . . talk about a hangover. Nothing will sink a credit rating faster than too many reckless Saturday afternoons at the mall.

We have a friend who had one of those power jobs to-die-for. Armed with an MBA from Stanford, "Dana" got a job managing the money of one of America's richest families. She flew all over the world managing their global investments. She hated the job, but with an income that left all of her friends in the dust, we were hardly the most sympathetic audience. When her job was eliminated, we assumed she would use the time off and her substantial severance package to pursue her dream of becoming the next John Grisham. Three months later she was flat broke and faxing her resumes to the local temp agencies.

Like me, Dana achieved the seemingly impossible: she squandered every last dime of her six-figure salary, forcing her to scramble for next month's rent. Dana took her compulsive shopping habits around the world with her. A rug in Spain, a spring wardrobe in Italy, antique glassware in London. Everything about her life looked glamorous until you saw her bank statement.

Now Dana's working at a job that pays a fraction of her old salary, and slowly getting back on her feet so she can take another crack at her novel. Don't you think Dana would trade those $1,100 Prada suits hanging in her closet for a chance to see her name on the *New York Times* bestseller list?

There are as many reasons for compulsive spending as there are excuses. Some people crave the false sense of empowerment shopping provides. Others use it to relieve boredom. Still others view it as a harmless vice and shrug it off as "retail therapy," a quick fix that ultimately can turn out to be seriously bad medicine.

People in their twenties are especially vulnerable to the lure of impulsive spending. As the most image-obsessed generation ever (after all, we came of age in the decade that gave us both MTV and designer jeans), we place a premium on appearances and consumer culture. Blame it on Madonna: as the "Material Girl" danced her way into our living rooms and our hearts, who knew she was actually picking our pockets?

THE THIRD DEBTLY SIN:
THOU SHALT NOT TRY TO KEEP UP WITH THE JONESES

Face it: we're genetically hardwired to compete with one another. Your fabulous coworker holidays in St. Barts and parties with Puff Daddy on New Year's. Do you really want to see the photos? No, you want to wallow in bitterness. It's a basic urge. We struggle for ways, some obvious, some not, to take us up a few notches on the social pecking order and give us a competitive advantage.

In our haste to win this race, we forget that not everyone gets off to the same start. Many people in their twenties have access to financial support that you don't (read: parents) or work in professions that simply move on a faster track. Struggling to keep up with every trust-fund baby or high school friend turned Ivy League corporate lawyer will cause you to make serious financial blunders you may regret for years to come.

You probably need to look no further than your own group of friends to see just how smart a strategy long-term planning is. Many of your frugal friends who passed on the expensive restaurants, the summer shares, and the extreme sports weekend getaways are probably homeowners now. Your more extravagant friends continue to flush the rent money down the toilet. Income has very little to do with it.

We have a friend who, despite his modest publishing salary, squirreled away enough money over the years to put a down payment on a small but elegant apartment. A year later he flipped it for a cool $30,000 profit. Compare that to another friend, a successful stylist, who spent every last dollar of her very comfortable salary dressing up her rental loft to look like something out of the pages of *Architectural Digest*. Her apartment is the envy of all her friends, but at thirty-eight she is no closer to owning her own apartment than the day she graduated from college.

It's not always just about competition; even good friends can become "debt enablers." By complimenting you on your latest extravagant acquisition and great taste, they unwittingly encourage financially destructive behavior. Any reservations you may have had about buying $400 titanium-framed glasses or spending $150 on a Frédéric Fekkai haircut are likely to vanish once you enter the room to a chorus of flattery. But that kind of praise comes with a serious price.

At a particularly tough time in my life, I bought an extremely expensive Italian leather jacket to cheer myself up. Now, I had no business spending the equivalent of three weeks' take-home pay on a jacket, but hey, I was depressed and I deserved it. Deep down, I knew it was a reckless and stupid thing to do, but with friends complimenting the jacket and asking to try it on, I was able to muffle the sensible voice inside my head that kept telling me to return it. It probably took a good year to pay off that jacket. Despite all the attention it got, I now wish a friend had pulled me aside and knocked some sense into me instead.

THE FOURTH DEBTLY SIN:
THOU SHALT NOT PRETEND TO BE TOO BUSY TO THINK ABOUT MONEY

Of all the excuses for not watching our money, this one is by far the most mind-boggling. When we tell ourselves, "I'm too busy living my life to deal with money," something does not compute. We all make time for what's important to us, whether it's going to the beach, spending a Friday night at a favorite bar, or racing home to catch *Survivor.* Unless you're a head of state or Martha Stewart, you're not too busy to manage your own money. But we use our own hectic schedules to mask deeper reasons for turning our backs on money.

When I made getting out of debt my number one priority, I became very conscious of every dollar coming and going. With a shock I realized that in the fifteen years of earning a paycheck this was the first time I had ever closely monitored my money. All those years, from high school to college and beyond, I treated money almost as an afterthought, a distraction to be dealt with as quickly as possible and then put out of mind. I lived the lifestyle I wanted, bought the things I desired, and didn't give much thought to how I would pay for it. With a shrug, I told myself that some way, somehow, the money would be there. I looked down on people who kept a close eye on their money. To me, they were money-hungry cheapskates who didn't know how to have a good time.

Determined to discover the roots of my feelings, I thought back to my earliest experiences with money. Growing up, my mother and her husband constantly told us kids what a financial burden we were. Seemingly every day they reminded us how much better their standard of living would be without us. I recalled all the times my stepfather sat glued to some financial show, while my mother posted the weekly supermarket receipts to the refrigerator door to let us know what it cost to feed us. They did without, and we were expected to do the same. While other kids in the neighborhood were showing off their new Atari video systems and Nikes, we were told to make do with what we had.

Much later I understood their motivations, but by that time all the guilt and resentment from my childhood had seeped into my subconscious and done its damage. Once out of the house and free from parental control, I rebelled. I was never going to let lack of money stand in the way of living the kind of life I wanted to lead. It seems crazy in hindsight, but all the anxiety, fear, and shame of debt seemed preferable to following in my parents' footsteps. I rejected their life of frugality and swung so far in the opposite direction that, after I strangled myself with debt, I became as obsessed with money as they were. Ironic, huh?

THE FIFTH DEBTLY SIN:
THOU SHALT NOT WASTE

A VH1 "Behind the Music" profile of MC Hammer revealed how the former rap star squandered virtually every penny he earned from his recording career. Now broke, the former baggy-pants aficionado recounted how he slowly bled millions on Trump-size shopping sprees that left him with a lot of toys and no way to pay for them.

It's tempting to dismiss cases like this as extreme, but the truth is there's a little Hammer in everyone. Most of us may not spend our money on ten-bedroom mansions and $80,000 cars, but neither do we have eight figures to burn. Instead we unnecessarily waste money because we're too lazy or afraid to sit down and consider better ways to use our money. Money we've worked hard for. Money that could be making more money. Money that, once gone, never comes back.

How often do you shell out $16.99 for a CD, listen to it once, and then banish it to the same shelf with the *Cardigans* and *Right Said Fred*? For all you dog owners out there who take Spot to be professionally groomed: why are you paying someone $400 a year for something you could do at home for free? That same $400 could easily cover a year's worth of electric bills. Gym bunnies, why do you spend $1 for a towel at the gym instead of bringing your own? If you work out three times a week, that's more than $150 a year. All because you can't be bothered to stick a towel in your bag!

Before you complain that all this cutting and trimming will whittle away your life to zero fun, chill. As we've said before, we know austerity plans fail. Getting a twenty-seven-year-old to take a vow of poverty, even a temporary one, is about as likely as

Keanu Reeves winning an Oscar for Best Actor—it's just not gonna happen. But you would be shocked at how easy it is to shake money out of your daily routine without asking your best friend to cut your hair or collecting government cheese. The money's there—you just have to know where to find it.

THE SIXTH DEBTLY SIN:
THOU SHALT NOT FORGET TO SET GOALS

Remember in high school when you staked a lifetime of future happiness on a thick letter postmarked from Cambridge, Mass., or a phone call from the cute girl in Physics? Okay, so you didn't get into Harvard and the next time you saw the cute girl, she was bald, tattooed, and on *America's Most Wanted*, but they were still goals, right? You knew exactly what you wanted, and you were prepared to do whatever it took to get it, even if it meant building a hospital in Honduras during your junior year just to have something to write about for your college essay.

Now, however, life's become a bit more complicated. Our dreams have grown bigger since then, and the path to achieving our goals is not as direct as it once was. It's a lot more fun to day-dream about financial goals than it is to work for them. A new car by twenty-five, a down payment for a house by thirty, early retirement by fifty—these things don't happen by themselves. It takes patience, planning, and a firm commitment to keep these goals front and center when temptation rears its head.

Unfortunately, at times our dreams can seem so unattainable we sabotage our future and settle for the consolation prize. I used to think saving enough money for a 20 percent down payment on a New York apartment was an impossible dream, so I didn't even try. Much later, I tallied all of the interest I had ever paid on my credit cards. I was devastated to discover that the interest alone would have covered not only the down payment, but a pretty nice house-warming party as well.

Not working toward a goal poses a double-edged jeopardy for the debtor: goals not only get obscured by a mountain of debt, but as the pile grows out of control, frustration mounts and it becomes all too tempting to throw up your hands, say "the hell with it," and go on an Imelda-size shopping binge from which you'll never recover.

We have a friend, "Elaine," who, between law school loans and credit card debt, owed more than $70,000. To someone making $45,000 a year, paying off $70,000 seems like an exercise in chasing windmills, so Elaine did what any of us would do: she ignored it. She bought $600 earrings, went diving in the Caribbean every winter, and owned every clever new personal electronic gadget on the market. She figured that since she could never hope to get out of debt, there was no point in trying. Her reasoning was understandable, but deeply flawed. A few years later she got a job that sent her salary soaring into the six figures, but her debt load kept her standard of living stagnant. Now she makes over $100,000 a year and has to explain to her parents why she still lives in a studio apartment every time they visit.

THE SEVENTH DEBTLY SIN:
THOU SHALT NOT BE RULED
BY YOUR SOCIAL LIFE

"Work hard. Play harder," a recent ad campaign urged. Good advice, and something that a generation that scoffs at a forty-hour work week as part-time should take to heart. But when we take a close look at the money many of us spend in pursuit of a little well-deserved R&R, a better slogan might be "Work hard. Play cheaper." Most of us would probably self-implode without fun in our lives, but if the money you spend pursuing the good life is wreaking havoc with your finances, then you're defeating the whole purpose of leisure time anyway. Look at it this way: if the

$50 you spend every Friday night at your favorite club is keeping you from chipping away at your debt, is three hours of loud music and watered-down beer worth all that long-term financial stress?

We're not suggesting you abandon your wild ways and become a recluse like J. D. Salinger. This is probably the only decade when you'll get to stumble in at 4:00 A.M. without feeling guilty. Once kids and a family enter the picture, you can probably count on fewer weekends hitting the slopes, too. And a life without fun isn't much of a life at all, right? We work to live, not the other way around. The challenge here is not to cut out play time, but to determine if too much of your income is going to leisure, and then find equally satisfying ways to spend less. If you are truly resourceful, you may find that you can rack up substantial savings and still be the weekend warrior we know you are. I will offer this embarrassing story as proof of how a little research beforehand can pay off big: One summer I decided I wanted to learn how to kayak. I went to a local sports complex and paid $165 for a four-hour training session and several half-hour guided outings at $30 a pop. When I mentioned my new passion to an acquaintance she asked me if I was aware of a municipal kayak club ten blocks away that offers free kayaking and lessons. Needless to say, I'm now a regular at the free place.

2

Go Figure

(or, Where Does

All the Money Go?)

TAKING YOUR FINANCIAL INVENTORY

There are three basic questions in life:

1. Is there a God?
2. Who thought "spray-on hair" was a good idea?
3. Where does all the money go?

It's a gruesome experience. You go to the ATM (for the fourth time this week) and withdraw another $60. You tear up the receipt before checking the balance or look away when it pops up on the screen. Money: sometimes it's easier not to think about it. And for most of us, it's a constant source of anxiety.

This is probably the biggest reason people find themselves swimming in debt—they can't deal. Most people don't really know where their money goes. A couple of dollars here, a rent check there, and poof! Your biweekly paycheck has vanished and you're forced to buy dinner on your credit cards. Again.

The first step is: Pay attention to your money. (We told you this would be easy.) To successfully rescue yourself from the malevolent clutches of debt, you just need to start thinking about the ways you spend money. Stop ignoring the issue. Check your balance each time you visit the ATM. Be aware of every dollar you spend. It's not something to get emotional or anxious about. Just think about it.

Here's a bit of advice that may surprise you: Stop feeling bad about spending money. We spend money every single day. No one can (or should) save every penny earned. Even if you prepare your own lunch, make your own clothes, live with your parents, and walk to work, there are still unavoidable costs of living.

When we budget our money, most of us think only about the obvious monthly stuff: rent or mortgage payments, car loan and insurance, student loans, credit card bills, utilities, and groceries. When we add these bills up, these expenses may seem ominous— but manageable.

But when you really think about it, we spend money in small ways—cappuccinos at Starbucks, magazines, a quick stop at the drugstore for shampoo, movies, parking tolls, bank fees—the list goes on and on and on. Most of the time these expenses don't really register. Sure, $8 for a movie doesn't seem like that much. But if you see 1 movie a week for 52 weeks, you've spent $416 (not to mention 52 weeks of popcorn and soda). Even spending 50 cents for the newspaper every day will set you back over $180 for the year. (More, if Sunday costs extra.)

Don't get the wrong idea. The solution here is not to become a penny-pinching miser; we simply want to help you get a hold on how much money you actually spend. In the not-so-magical art of managing your money, the truth really will set you free (from debt).

Why This Is Important

One of the keys to getting out of debt is prioritizing your spending. Think of getting out of debt as a war. You are a valiant soldier on the battleground facing off against the evil hoards from Visa, Sallie Mae, and the guy you borrowed fifty bucks from last week. These are your creditors (even that word is ugly), and your mission is to vanquish them by paying them off with your hard-earned cash.

To defeat these bad guys, you need a strategy. Like any good general, you need to start allocating your resources to where they are needed most. The money saved from a week's worth of dinners at home could pay off your monthly student loan. Or a ski trip planned for Colorado rather than the Swiss Alps could save you an extra $1,000—a sizable percentage of your Mastercard bill. Taking your lunch to work could save you $150 a month! That's *$1,800* a year!

When you know what you spend, strategizing your get-out-of-debt plan becomes easy. You'll have more money to spend on the stuff that's important by saving money on the stuff that's not. It was so easy for us, we wrote a book about it.

Obviously, there are some things we can't live without—food, shelter, and the occasional splurge at the mall. After you know your spending habits, you can begin prioritizing your spending. You will know exactly how you want to allocate your resources to best achieve our goal: get you out of debt, fast!

So how do I do this, anyway?

We can't stress this enough: Pay attention. You've got to know exactly what you spend so you can analyze your habits. You'll know what is essential and what you can easily do without.

The Real Deal: What You Really Spend Each Month

Now we're going to tabulate dollar for dollar what you spend every month. We promise this won't hurt (well, maybe just a little bit).

To make this process supereasy, we've divided your spending into three categories:

Fixed expenses: These are your monthly bills and fixed payments (like rent and car loans).

Variable expenses: These are your day-to-day out-of-pocket expenses. This includes lunch, cosmetics, movies, etc.

Occasional expenses: This is the random stuff—vacations, Christmas gifts, health club fees, and whatnot.

LISTEN UP! Budgeting Advice

Consider investing in home budgeting software!

Before you dig into our budgeting worksheet, maybe you should consider a small investment in a home budgeting program. Microsoft's Quicken is a good choice, and has special features that will allow you to automatically manage your bank account—so all the information is constantly updated. Also, Quicken's Turbo Tax will use all the information you input about your household budgeting to help prepare your annual tax returns.

FIXED EXPENSES

This is the big stuff, the modern-day basic necessities of life, the proverbial "things you can't live without." Now if you're living wildly beyond your means—driving a leased BMW to your job as a manager at the Gap—then it's time to make some tough decisions. You need to think realistically about getting a less expensive set of wheels or moving to a more reasonably priced pad.

But for most of us, it's the little things that sink us into debt. We drive a Honda, live in a decent, modest apartment, and then spend wild amounts of cash on clothes, cappuccinos, and crap. Unless you're willing to commute by bike or take in a roommate, it's generally difficult to immediately start saving money on "the big stuff." Also, for many of us, there are more and more "necessities" for modern living—things like cable TV and Internet service.

Provided that you're not in a serious cash crunch, we don't

advise canceling any of these basic services, selling your car, or moving. Getting a new car or moving requires a large outlay of cash—that's definitely the wrong direction. And for any upwardly mobile twentysomething, you gotta get E-mail, stay connected, and tune into VH-1 on cable. In twenty-first-century America, these things are arguably as important as water and electricity.

It is important to shop around for the best deal you can find, especially on things like Internet service. Most people would be surprised at how easy it is to find a better price on goods and services they buy. We'll talk more about this later. In a nutshell: just make sure you're not getting ripped off.

Okay, here's where the rubber hits the road. Sharpen a #2 pencil, relax, take a deep breath, find your happy place, and let's start thinking about your real cost of living.

The Bills

These are the basics, and probably the toughest place to save money (it's not like you can negotiate a better rate with the electric company). For truly ambitious types, there are ways to save money that you're probably not even aware of (insulating your house can save big bucks in the wintertime). But right now, just review your monthly bills and write down the amount of your last payment. If your bill varies wildly from month to month (perhaps your electric bill skyrockets from cranking up your air conditioner in the summer), try to find your last six to twelve statements and tabulate the average monthly bill. (Remember your second grade math? Add the amounts and then divide by the number of months.) If you don't have copies of your bills, you can request duplicates from your service provider.

YOUR MONTHLY BILLS

Rent or mortgage	$_____
Electric bill	_____
Heat	_____

Water _____
Gas _____
Cable TV _____
Phone service _____
Mobile phone service _____
Internet service _____
Other _____

TOTAL BILLS $_____

Transportation

In most American cities, if you had to make a choice between losing your legs or losing your car, the decision would be a no-brainer. Thanks to America's love affair with the automobile, most urban areas are an endless maze of pavement requiring residents to drive a car. This means loan payments, insurance, maintenance, and gasoline. (If you're fortunate enough to live in a city with decent public transportation, here's your chance to realize how lucky you are.)

YOUR TRANSPORTATION COSTS

Car payment $_____
Gasoline _____
Commuting costs
(tolls, garages, etc.) _____
Car insurance (If you pay
quarterly, divide by 3) _____
Car maintenance _____
Public transportation _____

TOTAL TRANSPORTATION $_____

Credit Cards, Loans, and Fees

Remember when you first signed up for a credit card? If you're like us, you were a freshman in college, naive and trusting. You got an application in the bookstore and you felt like someone just handed you $500 (my original credit line). A few semesters later you were stuck with a $3,000 balance and the dawning realization that you were never going to be able to pay it off. It's a living, breathing nightmare.

YOUR CREDIT CARD, LOAN, AND FEE COSTS

Bank fees	$_____
(Yep, you pay 'em. Check the fine print on your statement.)	
Visa	_____
Mastercard	_____
American Express	_____
Store credit card	_____
Other credit cards	_____
Personal loans	_____
Student loans	_____
Other loans	_____
TOTAL CREDIT CARDS, LOANS, AND FEES	$_____

Health Care

You gotta stay healthy to enjoy your newly acquired debt-free life. Enter the amount you spend monthly on health care. If you're one of the lucky ones, your employer may pick up the tab for most of this.

YOUR HEALTH CARE COSTS

Health insurance	$_____
Dental insurance	_____
Dental bills	_____
Prescription drugs/medicine	_____

Doctor visits   _____
Therapy   _____
Other   _____

TOTAL INSURANCE $_____

VARIABLE EXPENSES

This is where the real action starts.

Most of the time, we forget exactly what we spend our money on. The cash disappears in a haze of lunches, movies, drinks, magazines, trips to the drugstore, CDs, tolls, tips, etc., etc., etc. Every year you spend thousands and thousands and thousands of dollars without even noticing.

Until now.

Week to week, dollar to dollar, we're going to find out where you "dispose" of all of your "disposable" income. Since these are not fixed expenses, you may want to keep track of your spending over the course of a couple of weeks. One easy way to do this is to save receipts. This helps you keep a clear total of how much money is leaving your pocket on a regular basis.

Get a Calendar

An ordinary calendar can be one of your most effective tools in the war against debt. A daily diary of your spending habits is the best way to help you identify your spending patterns. The first step is to find a calendar and mark off the next fourteen days. At the end of each day, write down everything you spent money on that's not a fixed monthly expense like your phone bill or rent. These are your variable, day-to-day expenses: breakfast, morning newspaper, lunch, etc.

Here's an example:

20 Monday	21 Tuesday	22 Wednesday
Bagel + coffee $2.50	Grande Latte $3.50	Brunch w/ Colin $12.50
Gas $17.99	Newspaper $.50	
Dry cleaning $12.00	Haircut $22.00	Shirt at A+F $46.73
Lunch sandwich salad $9.27 Evian	Lunch at Cafe Habana $10.75 Tip $2.00	Wedding gift for Elizabeth + Bob $53.90
Dog food $5.23	Drugstore $24.13	Groceries $19.67
Dinner: Pizza w/ tip $13.00	Movie $6.75 popcorn/ Coke $6.00	3 Cosmos at Foxy $22.00
TOTAL: $59.99	TOTAL: $75.63	TOTAL: $154.80

YOUR WEEKLY SPENDING

Breakfast $_____
(Think of every bagel, muffin,
    coffee, or donut consumed)
Restaurants _____
Workday lunches _____
Groceries _____
Taxis _____
Laundry, dry cleaning _____
Cosmetics, toiletries _____
Magazines, newspapers, books _____
Pets, pet care _____
Bars or nightclubs _____
Hobbies _____
Movies or videotape rentals _____
Other _____

TOTAL WEEKLY EXPENSES $_____

Multiply this total by 4.5. (Remember, there are more than four weeks in a month.)

MONTHLY TOTAL $_____

OCCASIONAL EXPENSES

Here's the stuff that defies categorization. At the same time, it represents a lot of things we spend our money on. It's the random stuff. This may be a T-shirt from J.Crew or a long weekend in Florida. We ask for the monthly expenditures, so calculate the cost of the vacations you take over a year's time and divide by 12. (Do this for anything that's not easily quantifiable in monthly increments.) To jar your memory, you might find it useful to review old credit card statements.

YOUR OCCASIONAL EXPENSES

Clothes $_____

Vacations   _____

Gifts (think birthdays and
    holidays)   _____

Music (CDs, tapes, and
    concert tickets)   _____

Computer equipment or software   _____

Electronics (TV, VCR, stereo,
    phone, etc.)   _____

Membership fees (clubs,
    professional organizations)   _____

Charitable contributions   _____

Health club fees   _____

Home furnishings   _____

Home renovation or repair   _____

Moving expenses   _____

Other   _____

TOTAL OCCASIONAL
EXPENSES $_____

THAT ABOUT SUMS IT UP

You may want to sit down now. Add the total from each of the previous columns.

Total bills	$	_____
Total transportation		_____
Total credit cards, loans, and fees		_____
Total health care		_____
Total weekly expenses ($\times$ 4.5):		_____
Total occasional expenses		_____

MONTHLY EXPENSES
TOTAL $_____

Compare that to . . .

YOUR MONTHLY INCOME $_____

Pretty frightening, huh? Don't get depressed yet. Here's an anecdote that will cheer you up.

Karl's Story

After an assortment of postcollegiate odd-jobs, I landed my first real position as an assistant at a television network in New York City. Thanks to the triple threat of federal, state, and New York City income taxes, my take-home paycheck was $763 every two weeks. To make matters much, much worse, I was in serious debt. I had accrued a credit card balance of just over $8,000 by charging books, meals, clothes, and airline tickets during my four years in college.

I was depressed. Facing thousands of dollars in debt (compounding at 18 percent interest annually), I knew I had to do something. But with my relatively low salary, I didn't feel like I had the financial latitude to seriously attack my debt. That is, until I took a financial inventory, comparing

my income with my real expenses. This let me know
exactly how much money I had to pay off my seemingly
insurmountable debt. It also helped me create a realistic
timeline to achieve my goal of living debt-free. This was a
big psychological boost.

Since I was living in New York City, I faced certain
fixed expenses (e.g., exorbitant rent). Luckily, I had
two roommates to help me share the costs. This helped
considerably. My fixed expenses each month—rent
plus electric, gas, cable TV, and phone service—were
about $730.

Luckily for me, New York City has the finest public
transportation system in America (if you don't mind the
"aromatic" stench). To commute to and from work, I spent
approximately $70 each month. On top of this, I regularly
took cabs when I went out at night. When I added my cab
receipts up, this came to another $80–90 a month. (I was
shocked. I spent nearly $100 a month on cabs when the
subway was just two blocks away!)

But my credit cards were the real culprit. Four years of
books, beer, and pizza in college were being financed at
usurious interest rates. My minimum credit card payment
was $220 a month. Thanks to generous parents, I had only
one small college loan and my payment was relatively low.

After adding everything up, I discovered that just
by waking up in the morning I spent $1,110 monthly. I
calculated my monthly salary and realized I was bringing
home roughly $1,653. This gave me a monthly expendable
income of $543. Not much, huh?

I knew if I was going to really attack my debt, I'd have
to manage this money very shrewdly. The first thing I
needed to do was tabulate my variable expenses. Over the
course of two weeks, I wrote down on my little calendar
everything I bought—every bagel, magazine, cup of coffee,
whatever. Afterward, I calculated my monthly variable
expenses: $724!

Obviously, I was in trouble. I was already running a deficit without even factoring in the money I spent on things like clothing or the occasional vacation. Inevitably, my monthly overage was covered by—you guessed it—my credit card. This made my downward spiral into debt that much worse.

So trust me—if I did it, you can do it. Now don't you feel better? I survived to become debt-free. In the next few chapters, we'll show you how, too.

3

Setting Your

D-Day

Now it's time to pay the proverbial piper ... or the not-so-proverbial Visa, Mastercard, and Sallie Mae. In the last chapter we found out where your money goes; now we want to find out where your money *should* go. Here we'll take a look at all of your debts and plan the order of attack. Sometimes it's best to pay off those high-interest loans first. Or you may want to start on some smaller, low-interest loans to build that debt-free momentum.

First, we need to put you in the proper mindset for your new financially responsible lifestyle. Here are a few questions to measure your dedication to getting out of debt. Choose wisely! And remember class participation counts for a full 50 percent of your grade.

Scenario 1: The Tax Refund Cometh

Thanks to a super-savvy accountant, you get $1,400 back as your tax refund from Uncle Sam. What do you do with your sudden windfall?

a. Pay off your highest interest rate credit card immediately. You write "See you in Hell, Visa!" in the memo section.

  b. Reward yourself with a luxury vacation to Amsterdam to sample the local "culture." After sampling the "culture" you spend the rest of the money pigging-out at the local Burger King. Remember, over there a Whopper is called a "Royale with Cheese."

  c. Freak out! You thought you were going to get $1,800 back! You already spent the money on a kickin' home theater system Now you're really screwed.

Scenario 2: Final Markdown Moment of Truth

You're at your local stereo store and a system you've been jonesing for is on sale: "Final Markdown—40% off!" The only problem: you don't have the $450 it costs to take it home. What do you do?

  a. Resist the temptation because you already have a perfectly functional sound system. You spend the rest of the afternoon basking in glorious righteousness.

  b. You buy the stereo with your credit card after getting your credit limit raised . . . again. You take it home and lose the remote control in a week.

  c. Your friend distracts the security guards. You grab the display model and run like hell. Sadly you slip into a life as a petty criminal and end up doing hard time. Unfortunately, you find out prison doesn't have lots of singing and dancing like in that Elvis movie.

Scenario 3: The Mysterious, Magical Twenty Bucks

You slip on a pair of pants you rarely wear and discover *twenty dollars* hiding in the pocket. Oh happy day! How do you celebrate this serendipitous occasion?

  a. You save it for the grocery store and buy a week's worth of nutritious, healthy pasta, fruits, and vegetables. You invite your friends over for a pasta dinner.

b. You celebrate by going to the music store and buying $47 worth of CDs, including "Enya's Greatest Hits #2." You listen to it once, realize how much it sucks, and give it a new life as a $13 drink coaster.

c. You forget about it in your pocket until you get your pants back from the dry cleaners. You find a little shredded portrait of Andrew Jackson and spend the afternoon trying to rebuild him.

So, How Did You Do?

If you selected "a" for these scenarios, then you're in the right frame of mind to begin a serious plan of attack on your debt-ridden ways. You can skip to the next section and begin building your debt pyramid.

If you selected "b" for most of these scenarios, then you need to go back to your room and think long and hard about your commitment to getting out of debt. We can wait. We've got all the time in the world. When you're ready, answer the scenario questions again. If you consistently select "a," then you can proceed to the next section.

If you selected "c" for most of these scenarios, please turn back to chapter 1 and start again from the very beginning. Obviously you haven't taken us very seriously. We write and write and this is the thanks we get! You must have been a real treat as a kid.

STOP YOUR WHINING! DETERMINING WHAT YOU CAN SAVE EACH MONTH

In the last chapter, you determined your monthly income and expenses. Now it's time to think about where you can start to save. No one knows *you* better than *you*, and it's time to make some tough choices about where you can cut back.

Here's what you need to do:

- Record the monthly amount you spend on the expense listed.
- Determine if this is a necessary expense.
- Write down ways you might be able to save money on each expense.
- Determine if these savings ideas are feasible.
- Calculate how much money you'll save as a result.

We'll start you off with a couple of suggestions, but then you're on your own.

Savings Calculator

The following charts will determine how much money you can save to pay off your debt each month. (The examples in the first two rows should help you get started.)

Expense	Monthly amount (from chapter 2)	Necessary?	Ways to save	Feasible?	$ Savings
Rent	$630	Yes	Find a roommate	Yes	$315
Cable TV	$50	Not really	Cancel HBO	Yes	$20
Rent or mortgage					
Electricity					
Heat					
Water					
Gas					
Cable TV					

Expense	Monthly amount *(from chapter 2)*	Necessary?	Ways to save	Feasible?	$ Savings
Phone service					
Mobile phone					
Internet service					
Car payment					
Gasoline					
Commuting costs					
Car Insurance					
Car maintenance					
Public transportation					
Other					
Now add up everything in your "Savings" column. This is the amount you can save each month. →					

Now it's time to check out where you can save on your variable expenses. Remember: Cheaters never win! (Well, they *rarely* win.)

Variable Expenses

Expense	Monthly amount	Necessary?	Ways to save	Feasible?	$ Savings
Breakfast	$90 ($3 a day for 30 days)	You betcha	Eat at home	Yes	$40
Pet supplies	$20	Yes	Let Fluffy eat cake	No	$0
Breakfast					
Workday lunches					
Dinner/ Restaurants					
Groceries					
Taxis					
Laundry or dry cleaning					
Cosmetics/ toiletries					
Magazines, newspapers, books					
Pets and pet care					
Bars and night clubs					
Hobbies					
Movies or video-tape rentals					
Other					

Now add up everything in your "Savings" column. This is the amount you can save each month. →

Okay, we're almost there. Now it's time to think about ways to save on your occasional expenses. This is stuff like clothes, music, or vacations.

Occasional Expenses

Expense	Monthly Amount	Necessary?	Ways to save	Feasible?	$ Savings
Music (CDs, etc.)	$40 (3 CD)	Sort of	Borrow more CDs and tape them	Yes	$13 (Buy 1 less CD a month)
Health club	$80	Yep	Join cheaper club	Yes	$30
Clothes					
Vacations					
Gifts					
Music (CDs, etc.)					
Computer stuff					
Electronics					
Membership fees					
Charities (Sorry, wise-ass, you don't count.)					
Health club					
Home furnishings					
Home repair or renovation					
Moving expenses					
Now add up everything in your "Savings" column. This is the amount you can save each month. →					

Now let's see how much you can contribute toward your debt each month:

Total fixed expenses savings ➡	
Total variable expenses savings ➡	
Total occasional expenses savings ➡	
AMOUNT YOU CAN CONTRIBUTE TO RETIRE YOUR DEBT PER MONTH ➡	

CALCULATING SAVINGS:
One Woman's Painful Tale

Valerie just got out of graduate school and was mired in debt. "I had student loans, credit card debt, a car payment—I needed loans to pay off other loans. It was a mess." As an aspiring landscape architect, Valerie knew it would take a while for her salary to catch up to her talent, so she needed to make immediate lifestyle changes to begin dealing with her financial reality. She says, "I'd been living on the public dole for so long as a student, I kind of forgot how to be responsible and take care of myself."

She did a thorough financial inventory and determined where she could (and couldn't) save money each week. "Obviously, I had fixed expenses like my rent and student loans I couldn't touch." Since she lived in a city with decent public transportation (Boston), she decided to get rid of her four-wheeled beast: her car. "It was tough. I loved that car. But I saved almost $250 a month in parking, insurance, and maintenance for something that was pretty unnecessary." She also determined she could save money by canceling her cable TV ("All I watch is *The Simpsons* anyway."), eating breakfast at home, and taping friends' music collections instead of buying a lot of CDs. In total, she determined she could devote $350 to her debt each month. "After I totaled it up, I was pretty impressed. I had more money than I thought I would."

THINK LIKE AN EGYPTIAN: BUILDING YOUR PYRAMID OF DEBT

Okay, now it's time to prioritize. You can't possibly pay everything off at once, so now we're going to help you decide the best place to start attacking your debt. Think of your debt as a pyramid:

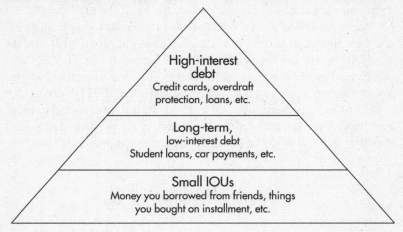

High-interest
debt
Credit cards, overdraft
protection, loans, etc.

Long-term,
low-interest debt
Student loans, car payments, etc.

Small IOUs
Money you borrowed from friends, things
you bought on installment, etc.

There are two ways you can begin attacking your debt, based on our pyramid approach:

- If you're paying 21 percent interest on your Visa card balance, then it's important to start paying this off as soon as possible. (Although there are exceptions to this strategy; see below.) You should commit all of your debt-reduction funds to your high-interest loans like credit cards and overdraft protection accounts.
- If your credit card bills just seem too massive, start to build momentum by paying off some small IOUs to get a few small debts out of the way. Turn your need for immediate gratification to your advantage. The larger sums may seem more manageable after you knock off some of the smaller loans. Start with a more modest installment loan or the $75 you owe your best friend.

The middle section of the pyramid is reserved for long-term, low-interest debt like student loans, car loans, or your home mortgage. Obviously, if you're carrying $80,000 in student loans then it's unlikely you'll be able to pay these off in the near future. Don't worry about it. These loans have much more favorable terms than credit card debt. As long as you're making your payments on time, then you should be okay while you take care of the other stuff.

Regardless, you should concentrate first on the top or bottom of the pyramid, depending on where you're at emotionally. If you're ready to tackle the big stuff first, then be our guest. If not, then start small to get the process in motion. It's less important where you start than *when* you start. Our suggestion: RIGHT NOW.

Here's your opportunity to build your own debt pyramid to help prioritize your payback plan. Write down all of your debts (remember doing this in the last chapter?) in the appropriate spot.

My Debt Pyramid

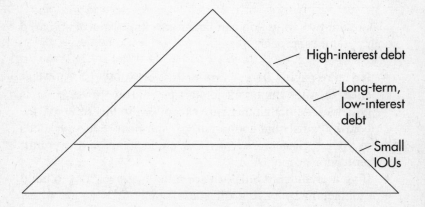

- High-interest debt
- Long-term, low-interest debt
- Small IOUs

The Power of the Pyramid

Bert was in a bind. His credit card debt exceeded $5,000, he had a monthly student loan payment, and he owed more than $400 to his friends and family. "I didn't know where to begin," he confided. "I made decent money, but I always just seemed to be scraping by." Bert made his own debt pyramid and used it to prioritize his attack.

"After analyzing all of my expenses and cutting back on my incidental spending, I calculated I had about $300 a month to devote solely to my debt. This was on top of the stuff I was already paying—like the minimum payment on my credit card." Since he owed so much to the dreaded Visa, he decided to pay off a couple of personal loans first. "I owed a friend $150. It started to be a strain on our friendship, because I never had the money to pay him back. I decided to start there." After paying off these small loans, Bert started on the big kahuna: his credit card debt.

He recalls, "I put it in a drawer and forgot about it. It was the only way to avoid temptation." He started sending the $300 along with his minimum payment of $120—a total of $420 each month. After he got a raise at work, he raised the payment to over $500. "Ten months later I got a Christmas bonus of $1,200. I used this money to finish paying off the card." In total, it took Bert about a year to pay off the debt. "Just think, if I would've invested that money I'd have over $5,000 now. What a waste."

JUST SAY NO! LIVING LESS LARGE

So now you know how much money you have to spend each month on your debt, and you know which debts to attack first. Now you need to start changing your psychology of spending. Before you buy anything, you should always be able to answer the following questions:

- *Do I need this?* Why are you buying this? Does it fulfill a physical, an educational, or an emotional need? For instance, a pair of shoes costing $80 might fulfill a physical need (everyone needs to wear shoes), but a pair of shoes costing $220 might be fulfilling an emotional need (I need a kick-ass pair of Prada loafers to make me feel special). You should understand your intention.

- *Can I get this cheaper?* Or can you buy something comparable that's less expensive? Most people buy things without thinking about simple alternatives. Have you checked out other stores? Have you tried to find a similar but less expensive version? Have you tried comparison shopping on the Internet?

- *How will this affect my debt-reduction plan?* You should always consider your debt-reduction plan when you make a purchase. If you're starting a new job and you need a suit you can't really afford right now, then this may be a legitimate expense on your credit card—but it will set your debt-reduction plan back a couple of months. Try to make sure that only genuinely necessary purchases interfere with your debt-reduction plan. Otherwise, this ain't gonna work.

Think, Think, THINK!

The lesson is simple: strategize your spending. Save money on the things you don't really want or need, and spend money on things you really (and we mean *really*) can't live without. There's a big difference between *want* and *need*. Unfortunately, we live in a culture increasingly ruled by the former.

It's important to step back and really analyze our consumption patterns to understand how much *enjoyment* we get out of the things we buy. We've developed a simple (unscientific and untested) way to quantify this gratification. Our Personal Enjoyment Inventory should help you prioritize your purchases. A caffeine freak may take it easy on new CDs, while a music lover will resist another $4 cappuccino.

Put a Price on Enjoyment

On a scale from 1 to 5, rate how much you enjoy the following popular cash drains. Give a "1" to those things you definitely *can* live without and a "5" to everything that is absolutely *essential* to your happiness on Earth.

PERSONAL ENJOYMENT INVENTORY

Eating out occasionally
   (1–2 times per week)   _____

Eating out regularly
   (≤4 times per week)   _____

Eating out chronically
   (4+ times per week)   _____

Your daily grind (pricey
   venti lattés, etc.)   _____

Designer styles (budget-busting
   clothes)   _____

Your ride (monthly car payment)   _____

Going out (drinks, dates,
   and movies)   _____

Mondo pricey music
   (CDs, minidiscs, etc.)   _____

gambling or playing Lotto
   (aka, Stupidity Tax)   _____

Out-of-town vacations
   (your two weeks of freedom)   _____

Now examine your list.

You should only spend money on things marked 1 and 2 when it's absolutely necessary. Redirect your expendable cash to the things marked 4 or 5. Everything else goes to paying off your debt (or after that, savings). For instance, if you're just as happy buying your clothes at the Salvation Army as at Saks, then do it. Spend less money on clothes and buy only when it becomes an essential. If

My Name Is Tina,
and I Am a Shopaholic

We put the word "practical" in the book's subtitle for a reason. For twentysomethings with limited financial experience, bailing yourself out of debt often requires nothing more than recognizing bad habits and learning how to spend smarter. For some people, however, killer debt is a symptom of deeper, psychological issues. If you feel this might be your situation, this book can still help you begin living a debt-free life, but you might consider seeking additional help to ensure you don't fall into those old, destructive ways again.

Consider the case of "Tina," a perennial graduate student and reformed debtor. "I was living on a pitiful stipend in Boston and I just could not live within my means. More to the point, I had no interest in trying. I ignored bills, defaulted on a store credit card, and soothed my anxiety by shopping. Eventually, my credit rating died on the operating table. I couldn't get another credit card, no bank would lend me money . . . I was scared and ashamed. Other people in my program managed just fine. I couldn't afford a therapist, so I started attending Debtor's Anonymous meetings. It took a while, but I finally got to the root of my problems. My mother had always demonstrated her approval with gifts and was very materialistic herself, so as an adult I subconsciously (sought) to repeat the same patterns."

Today Tina is gradually gaining control of her finances and can focus on more important things, such as finishing her thesis. If Tina's story rings close to home, you might consider seeing a therapist or attending a local chapter of Debtor's Anonymous. Look in the phone book for additional information.

you can't live without your flashy new convertible, then it's time to make cuts on your Saturday night social budget.

If you rated *everything* a 5, then the only thing you *need* is a shrink. Getting out of debt takes real commitment, and you've got to start saving someplace. Take another look at the list and start making some tough decisions. Will you really suffer if you don't eat out *every* night? We think not. After doing this exercise, most of us realize how unimportant most of our cash drains are to our overall happiness.

THE NEXT DAY OF THE REST OF YOUR LIFE: SETTING YOUR DEBT-FREE DATE

It's time to start setting specific goals for yourself. We want to choose a date where you'll no longer be a prisoner of debt. This is your D-Day. To stay motivated, you may want to have multiple dates: one for each major debt you need to repay. Also, if you buy something that's going to set back your debt-reduction plan, it's important to recalculate your D-Day.

But accomplishments come with rewards, right? We also want you to decide what you're going to do to treat yourself for your hard work, sacrifice, and determination. Try to be creative (and don't choose anything that's going to get you into trouble all over again).

Some suggestions: invite friends over for pizza, take a day trip to Amish country, experiment with bisexuality, or just get rip-roaring drunk. You have our permission to reward yourself—as long as you don't charge it on your credit card.

Follow the examples in our handy worksheet to help you determine your own D-Day dates.

Monthly debt contribution → (determined in the previous chart)				
Debt type	Amount	Monthly contribution	D-Day	Reward
Visa	$1,235	$145	April 20	Broadway tickets
Loan from Mom & Dad	$100	$100	Next week	Party all night, wake up with massive hangover
Amex Optima	$925	$100	December	New snowboard
Student loan	$5,000	$150	June 2004	One-night stand with best friend to satisfy curiosity

CHEAT SHEET

Okay, it's time for a quick review.

- *Determine how much you can devote toward your debt each month.* It's simple. Just write down the amount you spend monthly on each type of expense listed, determine whether it is a necessary expense, think of ways you might be able to save money on each expense, and decide if these savings ideas are feasible. The total amount you can save by making these changes will determine what you can spend on your debt each month.

- *Build your own debt pyramid.* It's important to prioritize your debt attack. If you're ready, try to attack your high-interest credit cards first. If this is too intimidating and you

---

Boys Just Wanna Have Fun

"I like any plan where I can reward myself," David explained enthusiastically. David had relatively minor debts—a couple of credit cards and some personal loans—but he could never motivate himself to get rid of them. "I only owed about $2,000 on credit cards, but I really couldn't bring myself to pay them off. There just always seemed to be something better to spend money on." David conducted his financial inventory, determined what he could contribute toward his debt each month, and completed his debt pyramid. "I didn't have any student loans, so I wanted to concentrate on my high-interest cards first." To encourage himself, David started planning a huge "D-Day Bacchanal." He smiled. "I decided to host a blow-out party to celebrate my financial independence."

David set a date eight months away. "I knew I'd look pretty stupid if I threw a party to celebrate something that never happened, so I hunkered down and really started paying off those credit cards. I even increased the amount of money each month, so I would definitely hit my target date." To further his resolve, David started making definite plans for his party. "I started inviting people and hired a bartender."

His dedication paid off. "I paid off my credit cards a month ahead of schedule." How was the party? David laughed. "I don't remember anything that happened—so it must have been good."

---

need a little psychological boost, consider paying off your small IOUs to start building momentum.

- *Prioritize your spending.* Be smarter about your spending. Direct your dollar to the things you love, economize on the things you don't.
- *Set your D-Day and reward yourself when you accomplish your goal.* Debt-reduction can be fun! (Okay, we don't even believe that.) It's important to establish milestones and reward yourself when you hit your target dates.

4

Found Money (or, Make Your Own Damn Frappuccino!)

We're starting a trend. Cheap is sexy. Your money goes further. More is less. People respect thrifty ingenuity.

This chapter explores simple strategies to help you save a bundle.

First, let's get to know you. Are you a spender or a saver? Chances are, since you bought this book, you fall firmly in the first category. Don't freak out, but it's time for the SAT: Savings Aptitude Test. Don't worry, it's only a "Yes or No" quiz. No math. We promise.

Savings Aptitude Test	That's me!	No, it's not!
I'm the kind of person who sneaks food into the movie theater.		
I'll split an entrée with a stranger to avoid paying for an entire meal.		
I know the exact price of everything I'm wearing right now.		
I try to compare prices on the Internet before I make any kind of major purchase.		

Savings Aptitude Test	That's me!	No, it's not!
I refuse to dry-clean if I can wash it myself.		
I never buy lottery tickets because I believe the odds are greater that I'll suddenly turn into solid gold.		
I rarely buy anything at a convenience store that I can get cheaper at the supermarket.		
I take public transportation because it's cheaper and better for the environment.		
I try to cook for myself at least four nights a week because it's cheaper and healthier.		
If I get a bonus at work I immediately pay off my debts or invest it in an interest-bearing account.		

YOUR SAT (SAVINGS APTITUDE TEST) SCORE

If you had between 7 and 10 "Yes" answers, then why did you buy this book in the first place? You know exactly how to conserve your cash. Maybe you can tutor some of the less fortunate, or spend the rest of this chapter resting quietly with your head down on your desk.

If you had between 3 and 6 "Yes" answers, then join the club. After reading this chapter, you'll know what you need to do to keep more of your money where it belongs: in your pocket. A few minor lifestyle changes can put you on the road to a cushy life of debt-free living.

If you had between 0 and 2 "Yes" answers, then you may be beyond all help. You should pay close attention to the advice that's being doled out in these next few pages. You're going to have to seriously rethink the way you spend money if you're going to get out from under that soul-crushing burden of debt.

THE MYSTERIOUS SECRET OF
DEBT-FREE LIVING REVEALED: SPEND LESS!

For most of us, our debt problems are not a function of how little (or much) money we make, but rather how much we spend. We all know someone who makes a decent income but is always short of cash. Similarly, everyone seems to have a friend with a more modest salary who's always flush. Many times the people with the most money are the most inept at managing it.

Want the simplest solution to your debt woes? *Spend less.*

Yes, Virginia, it's that simple. Now before you start moaning and throw this book across the room, think about this: we don't want you to stop spending any money, we just want you to get *more* for the money you do spend.

- How many times have you gone to your favorite store and found the same shirt you paid full-price for last week *on sale for $30 less*?
- How many times have you discovered that your friend's new stereo cost $120 *less* than your new *inferior* model?
- How many flights have you taken where the annoying, chatty person sitting next to you paid $300 *less* for his tickets?

Everyone can think of his own story where he got ripped off because he didn't know a better, less expensive way to purchase the same item. All money-wise people know: *retail is a four-letter word.* (Who suggested "Suggested Retail Price" anyway?) Saving hundreds of dollars on purchases can be as simple as waiting a few weeks for a sale or as easy as comparison shopping on the Internet. Just remember: every time you buy something, someone else is getting the same thing for less money. Be that person.

LISTEN UP! No-brainer Savings Advice

Take public transportation!

Our friend Todd is savvy, enlightened, and out to save the world. As a 23-year-old law student in Los Angeles he never considered taking the bus. He rationalized, "This is the epicenter of the auto culture, right?" A fellow student told him about a bus that stopped a block away from his apartment. "It seemed stupid not to at least try it." Todd found the bus went right to campus, took less time than driving (because he didn't have to park), and he saved big bucks. "I canceled my campus parking permit, which cost $120 a semester. Plus, I save money on gas." As an additional reward, Todd gets to feel morally superior to his less egalitarian classmates. "I consider that a bonus."

BE A CHEAP DATE:
ENTERTAIN YOURSELF FOR LESS

Going out on the town doesn't mean leaving your budget at home. Here are some fun and cheap ways to amuse yourself.

- *Rent a movie with friends.* This is exponentially cheaper than a night out at the movies. Try theme nights. An Elizabeth Berkley movie marathon is a surefire recipe for Fun! Fun! Fun!
- *Sleep.* One of life's great pleasures is also *free*! Instead of a lazy Saturday spent shopping, take a nap. Your body will thank you.
- *Exercise.* Good and good for you! Take the dog to the park, play frisbee with friends, or go out for a brisk walk. All of these things are *free*, and you'll feel better about yourself afterwards.
- *Instead of meeting friends for dinner, meet for coffee.* There are no excuses anymore. There's a coffee bar every twelve feet between Portland, Maine, and Portland, Oregon. Take

advantage of this trend by meeting your friends for (cheaper) coffee instead of a (pricey) meal.

- *Get off your ass and do something.* Volunteering for a charitable organization isn't only good for your karma, it's a cheap way to stay active and meet people.
- *Take up some kind of esoteric hobby.* Wouldn't you be a more interesting person if you started collecting something weird (but inexpensive) like snow globes or liquor bottles in the shape of former presidents? An eccentric hobby or collection is a cheap way to entertain yourself, and also a shortcut to popularity!
- *Go "antiquing."* "Antiquing" means you go to a lot of used furniture stores, look through a bunch of stuff that's not worth buying, and then go home empty-handed. (At least that's been my experience.) This is a cheap and entertaining way to kill an afternoon!
- *Pretend to be a foreign tourist in your city.* Visit your hometown's museums, science centers, or art galleries. Most of the institutions are heavily subsidized and therefore *cheap*! For added fun, pretend you're a confused foreign tourist. Ask bored museum guards, "Which way to the *Mona Lisa*?" It's a riot!
- *Take advantage of those book superstores.* Bookstores like Barnes and Noble can be a great (and cheap) way to spend the day. You can sit back in a big cushy chair and read magazines or books, and you don't even have to buy anything.
- *Get a boyfriend/girlfriend/partner/spouse (if you don't already have one).* Now this may be easier said than done, but nothing is more entertaining than the drama only a relationship can bring. Everyone knows how amusing other people's tragicomic relationship stories are. Why not experience this emotional rollercoaster firsthand! Plus, it's *free*!

SELF-CONTROL: NOT JUST
A LAURA BRANIGAN SONG

Controlling your spending and committing yourself to getting the best price is not going to be easy. It takes discipline and a bit of planning. But instead of concentrating on the sacrifices, focus on the benefits of your newfound thriftiness. Imagine buying a house, or taking a vacation—things made affordable by your financial ingenuity. Even better, imagine the rush you'll feel when you send the credit card company or student loan agency your final payment. Dream about what it'll be like to be *debt-free*!

One of the objectives of this book is to make you excited about saving money. Financial responsibility means more than just changing your lifestyle; it's a psychological mindset. When you finish this book, you won't be a complete cheapskate—but you'll cringe at the thought of wasting money. You'll thrill at knowing you're getting the most value for your hard-earned cash.

LISTEN UP! No-brainer Savings Advice

Buy department store *private-label* clothes and bedroom accessories! For basic clothing items like sweaters, socks, and shirts there's really not a lot of difference between designer clothes and the private-label lines that some department stores carry. Carlos, a friend of ours, works in the fashion business. "Believe me. I've been to the fabric mills in India. When those shirts come out they just slap a lot of different labels on them. Essentially, they're identical garments. It's amazing what some people will pay for a label."

MORE TIPS FOR KEEPING YOUR CASH

- *Don't play the lottery.* It's true, someone always wins. However, that *someone* will never be you.

- *The most lovable pets are also the cheapest.* It's sad, but some people put a price on love. Instead of adopting a lovable scalawag from the ASPCA, they insist on AKC-registered purebred dogs and cats with names like "Champion Lady Sire Ding Dong XII." People! Stop the madness! If you want a nonhuman companion, insist on rescuing a life from the shelter. (Jason's bulldog, who is just too cute for words, is the one permissible exception to this rule.)

- *Bah-humbug! Convert to avoid Christmas.* All right, this may be a bit drastic, but for lots of people Christmas is like the Super Bowl of bad financial decisions. Does Mom really need another Pottery Barn candle assortment? Will Dad really use that Sharper Image electric tie selector you paid ninety bucks for? Does Aunt Trudi really need another sausage assortment with whipped pimento cheese dip?

  One way to minimize the expense: have a family drawing. Each family member selects a name for another family member and only buys gifts for this person. It's easier. It's cheaper. And let's face it ... after five minutes with the family, all you really want is some more of that "special" eggnog.

LISTEN UP! No-brainer Savings Advice

Take care of your shoes!

Lots of people spend hundreds of dollars on shoes only to trash them in a few months. Jane, a 26-year-old account executive, discovered a quick and *cheap* way to prolong the life of one of her most treasured possessions: her footwear. "Now when I get a new pair of shoes I take them to the shoe repair shop before I even wear them." She has $5 sole-savers put onto every new pair of dress shoes. "It adds years to the shoes." She adds, "Plus, getting your shoes shined periodically will keep the leather from cracking and drying."

Now for some practical advice. Saving money isn't rocket science; you just gotta know where to start.

KISS THE COOK

Face it. Cooking sucks. And macaroni and cheese starts to get tired *fast*.

Food is one of our biggest expenses, but it's probably the one we think about the least. Ten bucks here, five bucks there—after a month, those pizzas, sandwiches, and Thai chicken salads really start to add up.

Do the math. If you spend $3 for a coffee and a bagel, $8 for a sandwich and a drink, and then $10–12 for dinner (these are all conservative estimates)—that's about $20 a day on food. Monthly this is around $600—which means you're eating (literally) $7,200 a year.

It's hard to face reality sometimes, but there's only one practical solution:

Start cooking at home.

Your Choice: Food or Shelter

Melissa was twenty-seven when she got married to Michael. They are a young couple with pretty normal aspirations—buy a house, have some kids, take a few vacations each year. "You know," she told me one afternoon, "the American dream." Their goal was to buy a house or apartment by the time they turned thirty. It didn't seem like an unreasonable aspiration for two ambitious young professionals.

However, Melissa and Michael never seemed to be able to save money. "We'd try to set some aside each month, but inevitably our checking account would become depleted before the end of the month. We'd have to take out money from our savings to cover our credit card bill and utility payments."

Melissa and Michael were confused. They didn't lead a

lavish lifestyle—a night out on the town was spent at the movies or visiting friends. "I couldn't figure out where the money was going," Melissa confided. They resolved to do a systematic review of their spending habits.

At first, nothing surprised them. Rent, utilities, and all their fixed costs were well within their expectations and budget. They totaled their incidental expenses—like movies, clothes, vacations. "I'm definitely more AnnTaylor than Armani," Melissa explained. "Neither Michael nor I would ever buy anything pricey or outrageous." Also, they lived in Chicago, so they didn't even have the expense of a car.

Finally, they totaled their food costs. They were shocked. "We both spent almost $30 a day eating out." Between breakfast at the deli on their way to work, lunch at the pricey sandwich place, and dinner at the cheap Italian restaurant around the corner from their apartment—they regularly spent almost $900 a month on food. "I knew if we ever wanted to buy a house we couldn't keep doing this."

Michael and Melissa started taking turns packing lunch. Forty dollars spent at the grocery store on the weekends could provide a week's worth of lunches. "Plus, the meals we made were just so much healthier. Everything you get out at restaurants is so heavy and the portions are so huge. We both looked and felt a lot better."

The money they saved went directly into their bank accounts. After two years, they'd saved more than enough money for a down payment on their house. Michael, an architect, is doing the renovations.

"Who knew that something that seems so insignificant can affect your finances so profoundly," Melissa mused. "By making one small sacrifice we were able to buy a house before any of our friends."

A cup of coffee at Starbucks costs $2. A half-pound of coffee at the grocery store costs $5—this will make you about fifty cups of joe. That's ten cents a cup and you don't have to feel guilty for not tipping.

Cooking is not as hard as it seems. Forget five-course meals and elaborate flambé extravanganzas—to develop good home-cooking habits you need to develop a repertoire of healthy recipes that are simple to prepare and easy to clean up. It's also helpful to make meals that can be stored and warmed-up later.

LISTEN UP! No-brainer Savings Advice

H_2O is good, and good for your wallet!

Before sucking down another syrupy sweet, tooth-rotting soft drink, try the delicious refreshment of tap water. Yes, water. With *zero* calories, *zero* sugar and *zero* fat . . . it's the world's perfect beverage, and doctors recommend drinking 6–8 glasses a day. Two soft drinks a day can add up to over $500 a year. It's a high price to pay for something that's just plain bad for you.

Good Recipes Are Like Good Dates: Cheap and Easy

We'll even help you get started on your quest for cheap eats. Here are some of our favorite easy recipes. Each one can be prepared in thirty minutes or less!

SPICY GRILLED CHICKEN

Cooking time: 24 minutes   *Cost per serving: $1.50*

2 tbl. cumin	1 tbl. brown sugar
2 tbl. paprika	1 tbl. red wine vinegar
1 tbl. pepper	2 crushed garlic cloves
1 tsp. salt	4 chicken breasts
1 tbl. brown mustard	2 tbl. oil

Combine cumin, paprika, brown sugar, pepper, curry, cayenne pepper, and salt. Stir in prepared brown mustard, red wine vinegar, and crushed garlic cloves; mix well. Rub chicken breasts with the spice mixture. Brush the grill with oil and place the chicken on the grill, skin side down. Cook over medium heat, about 10 to 12 minutes per side, until chicken is cooked through.

LISTEN UP! No-brainer Savings Advice

Forget the fancy $4 Frappuccino served by surly barristas! This homemade recipe costs a fraction of the price and actually (almost) tastes the same!

3 cups ice	1 cup chilled coffee
1 cup skim milk	Lots o' sugar
3 ounces condensed milk	

Blend like hell and voila! A frozen caffeinated taste of heaven. Total cost per glass: about 35 cents.

BLACK BEAN QUESADILLAS

Cooking time: 10 minutes   *Cost per serving: $1.40*

1 cup canned black beans	**1 tbl. cilantro, chopped**
2 tbl. green onions, sliced	**4 flour tortillas**
1 tbl. lime juice	**1 cup monterey jack cheese,**
1 green bell pepper	**grated**
2 tbl. red onion, chopped	

Mash canned black beans in a small bowl. Stir in sliced green onions, chopped green bell pepper, chopped red onion, lime juice, chopped cilantro, and crushed garlic clove; set aside. In a lightly greased skillet over medium-high heat, cook flour tortillas, one at a time, until softened, about 15 seconds each side. Divide grated

Monterey Jack cheese and the bean filling over the tortillas; fold in half; cook in the skillet for 2 minutes on each side, or until cheese melts.

FRENCH LENTIL SALAD WITH FETA

Cooking time: 25 minutes   *Cost per serving: $1.75*

3 tbl. olive oil   **⅛ tsp. salt**
2 tbl. vinegar   **⅛ tsp. pepper**
¼ tsp. thyme   **1 cup lentils**
¼ cup dried tomatoes   **1 cup feta cheese, crumbled**

In a large bowl, combine olive oil, vinegar, thyme, dried tomatoes, salt, and pepper. Place lentils in a saucepan, cover with water, and bring to a boil. Cook, barely simmering, until just tender, about 20 minutes. Drain and rinse. Combine with the olive oil dressing and top with crumbled feta cheese.

LOW-FAT BROWNIES

Cooking time: 28 minutes   *Cost per serving: $.70*

3 oz. baking chocolate   **3 egg whites**
1 cup sugar   **1 tsp. vanilla**
¾ cup flour   **¼ tsp. salt**
¾ cup low-fat yogurt   **¼ cup powdered sugar**

In a saucepan over low heat, melt baking chocolate. In a blender or food processor, puree sugar, flour, yogurt, egg whites, vanilla, and salt. Stir in the melted chocolate. Blend well. Pour into a lightly buttered 8″ baking pan. Bake at 350 degrees for 20 to 25 minutes or till the center is set. Sprinkle with powdered sugar. Cool. Cut into bars.

SPICY KEBABS

Cooking time: 30 minutes   *Cost per serving: $1.10*

2 pounds boneless chicken   **1 tsp. black peppercorns**
1 tbl. cumin   **1 tsp. salt, or more to taste**
1 tsp. cayenne

You will need a charcoal or gas grill and 12 to 15 metal skewers. Preheat grill. Cut chicken into small chunks, ½" across or less. Thread them onto skewers, without packing them too tightly together.

Grind or pound together the cumin, cayenne, and black peppercorns to a blended powder. Using your hands, rub spice mixture onto the skewered meat. Grill chicken for 5 to 8 minutes over hot coals. Halfway through the cooking, sprinkle the kebabs with a little salt.

Eating On-line

The Internet is a great resource for quick and healthy recipes. Here are a couple of sites that will make cooking a whole lot easier:

Meals.com. This site features over 12,000 recipes searchable by ingredient, type of meal, and diet restrictions. Meals.com even lets you save your favorite recipes and generates shopping lists so you know exactly what to buy the next time you go to the grocery store. Plus, the site will automatically scale recipes so you know how much to buy whether you're cooking for one or one hundred.

Foodtv.com. If you want to "kick it up a notch" with Emeril, Food Network features all of the popular cable network's recipes on Foodtv.com. The built-in search engine allows you to scan the site's database and find recipes from your favorite celebrity chefs.

LISTEN UP! No-brainer Savings Advice

Join a wholesale club!

If capitalism is a religion, then Costco is its church. Our friend Randy is a true believer. Every month he takes a trip to the wholesale club to stock up. "I buy all my staples there—cereal, detergent, light bulbs, orange juice . . . whatever." For a small membership fee (generally around $30) you can save close to 25 percent a year on your grocery bill. It's important to maintain perspective, Randy warns. "It's tempting to go crazy in there. Does anyone need five pounds of All Spice?"

RETAIL IS A DIRTY WORD

Before you buy anything, remember one simple rule: someone else is getting the exact same item for less. Much less. Most retail saving strategies are obvious. Always wait for sales. Pay cash so you're not stuck with credit card interest. Don't pay sales tax by ordering on-line or through a catalog.

Sales Tax Sneak

Some stores will let you save on sales tax by shipping your purchase to a state with no (or lower) sales tax. For instance, if you buy a $500 coat in New York, you can save the 7.5 percent tax by having the store ship your purchase to a friend in tax-free New Jersey. This is a great (and technically legal) way to save big on big-ticket items.

Don't Be an Idiot

Probably the best way to conserve your cash when you go shopping is to make a checklist of the things you actually need. How many times did you drop $60 on that perfect gray sweater, only to get home and realize you have three other *perfect* gray sweaters. Or you spend fourteen bucks on Depeche Mode's greatest hits album, only to discover all of those songs are already on CDs you own. It's probably the easiest way to feel like a complete idiot, right? Buying things we don't need—it's one of the most common mistakes made by money-foolish people.

LISTEN UP! No-brainer Savings Advice

Beware of outlet malls!

Here's an updated version of that old saying: "If something sounds like it's too good to be true, it's probably an outlet mall." As the outlet mall phenomenon has grown into a national obsession, prices have skyrocketed. You're often better off staying at home and hitting the sales at the local mall or department stores. These sale prices are just as cheap (or cheaper) than the outlet malls, and there's no fear that it will be shoddy "outlet-mall-only" merchandise.

Make a List

One sure way to avoid buying double is to make a list of the things you need—groceries, clothes, CDs. This is a smart way to coordinate your wardrobe or music collection *and* save a bundle.

Vintage Chic

Some of the trendiest threads and coolest home furnishings are as close as the nearest garage sale. Instead of dropping a couple hundred bucks on a particle board, cheapo dresser at Ikea, check out the local flea market or Salvation Army store. Most of the time the stuff is less expensive *and* of much better quality.

LISTEN UP! No-brainer Savings Advice

Forget the garage sale!

Before you start organizing the annual neighborhood garage sale, try to remember that the old Gap sweater you're selling for 50 cents could be donated to Goodwill or Salvation Army for an exponentially higher tax write-off.

Send Donatella Begging!

Ever notice how Club Monaco is just a rip-off of last season's Prada? It's easy to be fashion forward if you know where to look. Stores like Armani Exchange, Banana Republic, and J.Crew offer cost-conscious versions of more expensive designer items.

INTERNET SAVINGS

Between rent or a mortgage, electricity, gas, and water—your pad can start to be a serious cash drain. A dry, warm place to live is one of our basic human rights. Now, with that said, there are several ways you can cut down on your housing costs.

But it's a new economy, right? Traditional penny-pinching strategies are increasingly obsolete. It's all because of a little thing called . . . the Internet.

The Internet is probably the best way to save money since, well . . . ever. The best deals on airfare, clothes, electronics, groceries—anything and everything—are nothing more than a few clicks away. These days, you can't afford not to be Web-savvy. You may ask yourself: how do any of these sites make money? Our answer: We don't care!!! The advent of E-commerce created a shopper's paradise. You don't have to brave crowds, wait in line, or fight for a parking space. Sales taxes are nonexistent (in most areas). Many sites even have free shipping!

LISTEN UP! No-brainer Savings Advice

Get a free Internet service provider!

NetZero, www.netzero.com, offers *free* (you heard right!) Internet service for anyone willing to use a customized browser with dozens of sponsorship logos. If you don't mind the hard sell, you can save up to $250 a year.

Everyone knows on-line retailers like Amazon.com, CDNow, and Buy.com. These E-tailers have a reputation for low prices and deep discounts. But sometimes the much-hyped price savings are just that: hype. A smart shopper will know some simple ways to ensure he or she is getting the best price every time on the Net.

Lowermybills.com

Now this is really cool!

Lowermybills.com lets you automatically research, compare, and lower all of your recurring monthly bills—telephone, cellular, and Internet service, credit card rates, cable, loans, even insurance. You enter your information and then the site lists the rates for each available service provider. Then, with a couple of clicks, you can switch to the best deal. This is a great site when you're trying to select things like a long-distance telephone company. With all the competition now (even local phone companies can provide long-distance service), this is an easy way to make sure you're getting the most for your money.

Comparison Shopping Web Sites

Incredible. Amazing. These sites are the best tool for money-wise consumers since the invention of the "Going Out of Business" sale. The concept is simple. You input an item you want to purchase and a search engine scours dozens of on-line retailers—everything from toys to electronics to clothes to credit card rates.

A list appears with the name of the retailer and the price, and you click through to the best deal. *It's that easy!*

The only tricky part: it helps to know the exact name of the product you're looking for. If you want to buy a CD player, and simply type "CD player"—you'll end up with thousands of selections. You may want to do a little research beforehand to find the exact model you want to buy. This will make it easier to get useful results.

We did some searches to demonstrate how great the savings can be on a variety of items. Check out some of our savings.

Internet Comparison Shopping Site Results

Product	Price	Site
Sony DVD Player	$399.00	Buy.com
	$269.00	Best Stop Digital
	$259.00	Supreme Video & Electronics

Pretty amazing, huh? For 30 seconds of work we saved $140.

CDs are one of our favorite things to order on-line. What did our search turn up for a Fiona Apple album?

Product	Price	Site
Fiona Apple CD	$12.94	800.com
	$15.99	BestPrices.com
	$12.58	Amazon.com
	$9.90	Mymusic.com

$9.90—they're practically giving Fiona away! Pity the poor soul who went to the misleading named "BestPrices.com" and paid over $6.00 more for the same CD.

Product	Price	Site
Prince Precision Tennis Racket	$124.20	Tennis Warehouse
	$159.95	Midwest Sports

Sports fans! Here's a deal we found on a tennis racket. Grand slam! We just saved over $35.

Unfortunately, these comparison shopping sites don't account for add-ons like shipping (which some sites provide for free). You should check out the two lowest prices and compare the actual total after the price is adjusted for shipping and taxes.

Here are two comparison Web sites we recommend.

MySimon.com: This site features a creepy animated character named Simon who acts as your helper and host. The site is intuitive and easy to use, and features direct links to product-specific categories. The site searches over two thousand different on-line merchants, and almost every item we searched listed three or four different prices.

MySimon.com offers a free e-mail newsletter featuring shopping tips, product profiles, and so on. You can also register for free membership in the MySimon.com shopper's club. As a member, the site will automatically monitor a set of pre-selected items and send you an E-mail when the product is listed at your specified price.

Dealtime.com: Dealtime.com works exactly the same way as MySimon.com. You enter an item, and the site searches the Internet for the best price. The only difference is Dealtime.com also searches auction sites like Ebay, Ubid, and Yahoo Auctions. This means you can comparison shop for everything from DVD players to collectible baseball cards.

Dealtime.com improves on MySimon with its free notification software. Instead of sending you an E-mail with updates on pre-selected items, Dealtime.com installs an icon on your desktop. Anytime there's new price info about a product you want to buy (this also offers updates on stock prices and news stories) the icon flashes. When you click it, Dealtime.com launches your Web browser and takes you to the information you've requested.

Auction Sites

Looking for a great deal on a 1978 Bee Gees LP? Auction sites are one of the Internet's best innovations. These sites are simple to use. You search for the item you want to buy (Ebay lists almost four million items for sale!). Enter the price you're willing to pay, and if you're the highest bidder—you win! The seller of the item will contact you with address information and you drop a check in the mail.

How do you know you're not going to get ripped off? Good question. On Ebay, each seller is evaluated by previous customers for reliability, truthfulness, etc. Also, with each purchase you're insured up to $200 (minus a $25 deductible), so Ebay will help pick up the tab if you get screwed. Ubid is different. On this site you deal with the company directly, so this transaction is as safe as any other on-line retailer.

Auction sites are great resources for collectors, but they're also good for finding great deals on new (or almost new) items like computers, stereos, and TVs.

Ebay.com: This is the Mama Bear of all auction sites (and if you bought Ebay's stock at its IPO, you definitely don't need this book). The site is simple to use and features almost every conceivable item for sale—everything from a James Dean cookie jar to a brand new JVC camcorder. You can even make a bid on used underwear, if that's your thing. It's true. Check it out.

Ubid.com: Ubid works exactly like Ebay except the items for auction are all new. This site is a way for companies to sell overstocked merchandise. Deals abound—we found a Compaq color-display notebook computer for $1,000. All items are shipped directly from Ubid, so deliveries and returns are easy.

"Name Your Price" Sites

Priceline.com: For shopping on-line, Priceline is really in a category all its own. This site lets you "name your price" for everything from airline tickets to hotel rooms to groceries to rental cars to home mortgages. The process is a little cumbersome. For airline tickets and hotel rooms, you enter the amount you're willing to pay and the dates you're willing to travel. Here's the catch: if you're bid is accepted, then Priceline automatically charges your credit card. Also, for airline tickets you can't select a specific time to travel, so you may find yourself on a 6:00 A.M. flight. For groceries, you simply enter the price you're willing to pay for each product. Priceline provides a list of your accepted bids, and then you take it to a participating grocery store to pick up your items.

Sound complicated? It is. But a little work can add up to extraordinary savings. A friend of ours landed two tickets to Amsterdam from New York for only $175 apiece. Another friend who buys her groceries using Priceline regularly saves up to 40 percent on her food tab.

Buying Cooperatives

These sites offer cool discounts on products by arranging group discounts. You simply find the product you want to buy, and the site lets you know how many orders it needs to fulfill the order at a specific low price. Once a set number of customers order the product, your credit card is charged and the product is shipped. The only problem: if there are not enough orders the transaction won't go through.

Mercata.com: This is the most well-established of the on-line buying cooperatives. The product list is extensive, featuring electronics, kitchenware, sporting goods, and more. How good are the deals? We found an Arnell Snowboard for $154—that's almost $100 cheaper than the retail price. Also, the more customers who register to buy an item, the lower the price.

The Dark Side of Dot Com

Our friend Reed had a problem: he was a dot com junkie. "I spent at least a couple hours at work each day surfing shopping sites on the Internet. 'One-click' shopping on Amazon.com really became a problem for me."

Reed would regularly spend over $100 a month on CDs he ordered on-line. The ease and availability of on-line shopping, coupled with a job with fast Internet access, made every day at work like a trip to the mall. "It was really becoming a problem."

This is the dark side of dot com. Sure, it's easy and convenient. But for a lot of us who spend massive amounts of time sitting at a computer at work, it can rapidly become an expensive addiction.

Here are a few tips you can use to avoid dot com disaster:

- *Turn off "one-click" shopping.* They make it easy for a reason— they want you to spend, spend, spend! They know you'll be much more inclined to buy the new Stephen King thriller if you're only a click away.

  Try to make the experience as inconvenient as possible by turning off "one-click" shopping on your favorite sites. If you know you're going to have to type in your address and credit card number, you'll think twice before an impulse purchase.

- *Don't shop for entertainment.* Many of us spend hours browsing on-line shopping sites just for the entertainment value. Sometimes this can be pretty innocuous—like pricing your first-class fantasy vacation on Travelocity to Ulan Bator.

  And sometimes you can end up with 10 CDs, a digital camera, and Jewel's new book of "poetry." It's best to only visit shopping sites when you know what you want to buy beforehand. Get in and get out—quick!

- *Trash your browser.* Okay, this is pretty drastic. But if you really can't control yourself, this may be your only option. Drag your browser into the trash before it's too late!

On-line Travel

The Internet has revolutionized the travel industry. For budget-sensitive twentysomethings, on-line travel reservations are the quickest, easiest, and cheapest way to get out of town. Travel Web sites let you compare rates, times, airlines, and schedules to make sure you're getting the best deal every time.

These travel sites are two of our favorites:

Travelocity.com: Travelocity is the grand-daddy of travel sites. You can book a flight, a hotel room, car rental, a package vacation, even a cruise. One cool feature: Travelocity will monitor pre-selected flights and automatically send you updates about low-fare deals. Membership is free, and your customer profile stores all your frequent flier information, credit card numbers, even meal preferences.

Cheaptickets.com: Cheaptickets is a bit clunkier than Travelocity, but the site functions in a way that makes it a bit easier to find low-priced tickets. Instead of listing the lowest fares for the flights you select, it simply shows you the entire fare structure for your selected flight. This means that even if the lowest fare available for your Atlanta to Miami flight is $236, Cheaptickets will show you the cheapest published fare of $89. You then have to do a little legwork to adjust your flight schedule to find that available fare.

Check out how much money we saved on these trips:

	Travelocity	Cheaptickets	Airline 800#	Savings!
TWA Los Angeles– Miami (14-day advance)	$354	$342	$581	**$239**
Northwest New Orleans– Seattle (14-day advance)	$224	$240	$360	**$136**

LISTEN UP! No-brainer Savings Advice

Don't touch anything when you stay at a hotel!

The phone? Don't touch it. The minibar? Don't touch it. The Spectravision? Don't touch it. Your average hotel room is like some kind of alternate universe where everything costs 400 percent more once you walk through the doorway. Use a lobby pay phone or your one-rate cell phone to avoid call charges (as high as $1 per call just for dialing the phone). Don't pay $9 to see *I Dreamed of Africa* on pay-per-view. And before you open up that $4 bag of nuts, just remember the same bag of nuts is available elsewhere for 89 cents. Your hotel room is for sleeping, not shopping.

Remember! Always try to keep your schedule flexible when looking for the lowest fare. Sometimes you can save hundreds of dollars by taking an early afternoon rather than a morning flight. A bit of research will pay off every time.

IF YOU THINK IGNORANCE IS EXPENSIVE, TRY EDUCATION: STUDENT LOANS

You may ask why we've included student loans, the bane of many twentsomethings' existence, in Found Money. Good question. The answer? We couldn't figure out where else to put it!

Unlike most debt we carry, you needn't feel one iota of regret for your student loan burden. The U.S. Constitution guarantees the pursuit of life, liberty, and happiness. It says nothing about a free ride at Stanford. College is a hugely expensive proposition for many families, and student loans make it possible for a lot of people who would never be able to afford it through scholarships and parents alone. Unfortunately, though you may forget your college French soon after they hand you your diploma, you may be paying for those classes for the next ten years if you carry heavy loans.

There aren't too many ways to seriously slash the cost of your educational debts. You are still responsible for them if you declare bankruptcy and you can't negotiate a lower rate with your lender. However, there are a few things you can do to make the cost of the loan more manageable:

- *Consolidate your loans.* The Federal Direct Consolidation Loan Program allows you to combine all of your loans into one with a single, low rate. The rate will vary, but there's currently an 8.25 percent cap on the interest rate. Other servicers offer competitive consolidation rates as well. Try calling the Student Loan Marketing Association (Sallie Mae) at 800-643-0040 to see if you're eligible.
- *Sign up for automatic debiting.* You have to write a check every month anyway, so why not have the money automatically deducted from your account and save a little on interest. Sallie Mae will shave off a quarter point if you authorize them to deduct the money from your bank account automatically. To get started, all you have to do is sign an authorization form and send them a canceled check.
- *Delay repayment.* If you're drowning in high-interest consumer debt, it may make sense for you to take a break from your lower interest student loans until you get your financial situation under control. You will usually, though not always, still be responsible for the interest during the deferment period. For more information, contact your loan servicer. (Warning: Generally, deferments are not granted because you "needed" a new $28,000 sports car and now can't keep up with the payments. You might have to fudge your reasons for requesting the deferral.)

Cheat Sheet

Saving money isn't tough. The most difficult part is breaking our bad habits and refusing to rationalize our wasteful ways.

- *Pay attention.* Think about every dollar you spend by keeping a mental (or written) tabulation of your daily cash outlay. The results will surprise you.
- *Forget retail.* Be the person who gets the best price on everything. Shop only during sales or at warehouse stores or discounters.
- *Cook at home.* Eating out is a major cash drain. Cook at home for big $$$ savings.
- *Use the bargain hunter's best weapon: the Internet.* The Internet makes comparison shopping a breeze. Always check on-line to make sure you're getting the best deal. (But beware the pitfalls as well. Don't go dot com crazy.)
- *Don't feel guilty about student loans.* Education is the smartest way you can invest in yourself. Consider consolidating your loans and signing up for an automatic debit plan to reduce your interest rate.

5

Death by

Plastic

For many of us, credit cards represent ground zero of our financial troubles. Before student loans, backbreaking rents, and 40 percent tax brackets came that first piece of laminated plastic peeking out of the dorm mailbox. If you carry a lot of credit card debt, you probably find it interrupting your most peaceful moments—when you're on the treadmill, out walking the dog, or driving home from work. Your obsession with getting into the right college has been replaced in your twenties by fantasies of a zero balance.

Credit card companies are slick operators. They're not so different from Vegas casino owners—for all the tantalizing promises they dangle in front of you, the odds always favor the house. After all, they are in this business to make money, and they will go to great lengths to keep your balances high and your payments low. However, you, as a cardholder, have a few tricks up your sleeve as well. In this chapter, we show you how to arm yourself against these money-sucking Goliaths and save hundreds, if not thousands, of dollars a year. The money you save can go a long way toward knocking down those seemingly unconquerable balances. Used cautiously, credit cards are one of the greatest inventions of the twentieth century—up there with the computer and low-fat baked potato chips. Used recklessly, however, they become a weapon of mass destruction—to your credit rating, your saving plans, and your general happiness. But we probably don't have to tell *you* that.

PLASTIC 101

Whether you've been violated by Visa or assaulted by American Express, paring down your plastic is the first step toward credit card liberation. Many credit counselors advocate cutting up all of your cards and using cash for everything. While this may have worked fine for our less-evolved ancestors, frankly, we think that's unrealistic today. Unless you're planning to join the Amish, you will need at least one credit card to keep life running hassle-free. If you doubt us, try ordering something on-line without one.

Below we list the common types of cards most likely to be found in your wallet and describe the most important features to consider when evaluating whether a card is right for you.

Credit Cards

A card that allows you to carry a month-to-month balance is called a credit card. Visa and Mastercard are the two biggest, but the Optima card is widely held among young people as well. Discover, which is issued by Sears, works the same way as these other cards, but it is far less popular with the twentysomethings.

Each month when you receive your statement you have the option of paying the *minimum payment*, the full balance, or any amount in between. Any unpaid balance accrues interest at either a variable or a fixed interest rate that usually appears at the bottom of the statement.

Charge Cards

A charge card requires you to pay off your balance in full each month. These cards offer convenience only, not long-term loans

like their Visa and Mastercard peers. American Express is the
most widely held charge card, but there are others.

The biggest advantage these cards offer people with undisci-
plined spending habits is that the balance must be paid in full each
month. Skip too many payments and you can expect a cranky letter from the home office. Speaking from experience, these people
don't mess around. I remember getting a nasty letter from Amex
my freshman year, inquiring why I hadn't responded to any of
their repeated phone messages. The letter ended with the unforgiv-
able line "The American Express Card is not for everyone." Two
days later, they unceremoniously canceled my card.

This tough-love attitude can encourage you to stay on your issuer's good side, but there is a potential downside. If you do freelance work and/or your main source of income is unsteady, you are
better off with the flexible repayment schedule of a credit card to
get you through the dry spells. Similarly, if you have an expense
account and you work for a company that takes an eternity to reimburse you (like a Hollywood studio, for example), you might
find yourself facing a large bill at the end of the month as your expense report sits in some Burbank bureaucrat's in-box.

Store and Gas Cards

If you already have a credit card, there is really no reason to
carry these other cards. There is practically no store or gas station
on earth that accepts only its own card, and the interest rates these
cards charge are generally higher than a credit card. Also, for
some reason many people don't take store debt as seriously as
other forms of debt, so the temptation to take one in every color
can prove too tempting too resist. If you are one of those people,
steer clear of salespeople offering immediate approval.

There is one benefit to these cards. If you don't have a credit
record because you are just starting out, store cards offer a convenient way to establish credit since they're easy to get. Our suggestion: Get a store card, pay your bills on time for six months, then
cancel it and get a standard one.

Debit and Secured Cards

Many people who use these cards often do so as a last resort, but they can also be great tools for preventing you from spending money you don't have. Both are usually issued by banks or credit unions under the Visa and Mastercard names, which means no one can tell you're not using a true credit card.

With a debit card, you simply deposit money into an account, and each time you use the card, the money is deducted directly from that account. You can add money to the account any time you like, and, best of all, you will never have to worry about being unable to make a payment or abhorrent interest rates. Just shop around for the best deal, as many institutions will try to sneak in high annual fees.

For the truly credit-scarred, a secured card may be your only option. A secured card works more like a traditional credit card, but here the issuer requires a guarantee that you have the money on hand should you default on your balance. You must set up a special savings account that you cannot touch as long as you carry the secured credit card. The bank will usually allow you to carry a balance equal to or slightly greater than the money in the account. You must be very careful when choosing a bank. Even with the collateral of a savings account, many banks will use your spotty credit history as an excuse to charge higher interest rates than a traditional credit card.

How They Make Money (and How You Waste Yours)

Interest

If you've ever been driven to tears by the finance charges at the bottom of your statement, you already know the answer to this question. Banks levy interest on your unpaid balance at interest rates that can quite easily surpass your age. (Sucker rates of 24 percent are becoming increasingly common, once again proving P. T. Barnum knew what he was talking about.) The rates appear two ways. The *periodic rate*, which is the interest rate your balance is subjected to daily, appears as a harmless-looking figure with all the numbers after the decimal point (such as .05476 percent). This sounds like a great deal until you glance at the *annual percentage rate* (APR), which is simply the periodic rate times 365. That is the yearly rate of interest your card carries. In the case of the periodic rate above, the APR translates to 19.99 percent. Suddenly that little number looks a lot less innocent.

Interest is how the banks make their money. The average card carries an interest rate of about 17.5 percent. The government lends the banks money at a rate of about 5 percent. That 12.5 percent difference between the two rates represents almost pure profit (unless you deduct the cost of all those commercials featuring really attractive people impulsively charging lobster dinners on Nantucket).

As if that weren't bad enough, banks calculate interest in ways designed to keep you in the hole as long as possible. If you pay off your balance each month (which the vast majority of us do not), you can avoid interest charges. Most banks offer a *grace period*, which is the number of days you have to pay your balance in full before interest charges kick in. However, if you carry a balance of even a dollar, you lose that grace period and any new charges begin accruing interest immediately. In real terms that means that if you charge a pair of $100 shoes on a card with a balance, those shoes become more expensive by the day.

Complicating matters even more is the *average daily balance* system of calculating interest. Most banks use this method, and it's not difficult to see why. Say, for example, you decide to pay off an old balance of $2,800, and you send a full payment a week before the due date. Your next statement should read $0, right? Wrong. That $2,800 has been accruing interest every day between the time you received your statement and the date your payment is credited. You would owe about another $46 in interest, even though you sent the payment in on time. Now you understand why it's so difficult to pay off those damn balances.

Fees

Years ago cardholders had only one fee to contend with, an annual "membership" fee that, when you think about it, doesn't really make much sense. Banks justify the annual fee by claiming it covers expenses such as processing and mailing costs, but don't believe it. Banks receive a percentage of every purchase you put on the card (usually between 1.5 and 5 percent) that more than covers their costs. Essentially, the credit card companies are asking you to pay a tax for the opportunity to make them money. Imagine if your favorite store started charging a fee just for walking in the door. You'd find another favorite store pretty fast, wouldn't you?

Today, however, as banks look for ever more creative ways to separate customers from their dollars, they've initiated even more obnoxious fees. Miss the payment deadline by one day and many companies will slap you with a late fee ranging from $15 to $30. (Some cards will even use a single late payment as an excuse to raise your interest rate.) If you go over your limit by just $1 you may be penalized with an over-the-limit fee each month you're over. More galling, certain credit card companies have taken to punishing responsible cardholders who pay their balances in full each month! You have to admire them for their nerve.

With all the cutthroat competition out there among credit card companies, there is almost no reason you should pay these fees, membership or otherwise. Dozens of banks offer no fee cards, and even if you don't find one to suit your needs, you have a good shot at waiving an existing fee simply by asking nicely. Of course the easiest way to avoid late fees is to pay on time, even if it is just the minimum. (It's also healthier for your credit report.) But if for some reason you miss a payment, don't be afraid to fight. Lie if you must (two personal favorites: "I was on vacation the weekend of the payment date, so I couldn't mail it in," and the old standby, "it got lost in the mail"), but remember, very few credit card companies are willing to lose a good customer over a late fee.

Paying the Minimum Payment— What Are You Thinking?

For credit card users (that means you), there are two prices for everything. There's the listed price—this is the price of an item you pay in cash. And then there's the credit card price—this is the amount you really pay after factoring in interest.

Now if you're only sending the minimum payment, you're (excuse our French) really getting screwed. Most credit card companies calculate the minimum payment as 2 percent of your average daily balance or $10—whichever is greater. With interest continually compounding this means you'll end up paying off your credit card . . . well, never.

If you insist on sending only the minimum payment, here's the real price of some stuff you just might have charged in the not-too-distant past.

2 percent minimum payment at 19.8 percent APR

Item	Price	Interest	Total	Years to Pay Off
iMac	$1,200	5,065	6,265	29.6
Hugo Boss suit	700	2,208	2,908	16.8
Tag Heuer watch	875	3,207	4,082	22.1
Palm Pilot	400	659	1,059	5.4
Paris vacation	2,300	11,351	13,651	45.1

Forty-five years! Sacre Bleu!
(calculator courtesy myvesta.org)

Three Ways to Reduce Your Payments

Even if you don't currently have the cash to take a big bite out of your credit card debt, lowering your interest rates *now* can go a long way in keeping your balances in check. Most people either don't know they can negotiate with their credit card company or don't realize how substantial their savings can be. As you can see from the tips below, all it takes is a phone and a little nerve to drastically slash those finance charges.

Ask for a Lower Rate

You'd be surprised at how receptive banks are to lowering their rates to keep a good customer. This is partially because the credit card market is so fiercely competitive that they can't afford to lose you, and also because credit cards operate on such high profit margins they can still cut their rates and make money. You have two ways to approach this. The first is to call customer service and say that you are thinking of switching to a card with a lower rate. (Be sure you actually know of another card with better terms because you may be asked.) Let them know you mean business, but be polite. Threats and foul language, while often deserved, are not advised.

The second approach usually yields more dramatic results, but requires both a little acting ability and a willingness to lie—er, exaggerate. This time when you call customer service, claim financial duress and express concern that you may have difficulty making your payments. Banks live in white-knuckled fear of calls like this, because defaults and delinquent accounts cost them millions of dollars each year in write-offs and legal fees. It is much cheaper for them to help you through a rough patch than to come after you in bankruptcy court. I know a co-worker who did this and got his rate lowered to 5.9 percent. I tried it and got 6.9 percent. (I guess he was a better actor, but it still beat the 19.8 percent I was paying.) Just keep in mind, however, that banks will grant these "relief" rates for a limited time period (usually no more than six months). And no, this won't hurt your credit rating.

Consolidate Your Individual Credit Card Balances

Now that you've got this great new interest rate, don't be shy about taking it for a spin. If you have enough credit available and your account is in good standing, your bank should allow you to transfer other card balances to this card. Besides the savings in interest, shoveling all of your little debt piles into one has another important benefit. It becomes much easier to track your progress in debt-reduction, and allows you to focus your energy on a single target. Other balances can't creep up on you when your back is turned. It's kind of like aiming a firehose on one big fire instead of trying to stamp out a bunch of little ones—you extinguish the problem before it gets a chance to reignite.

Credit Card Surfing

Banks are generally much more willing to work with you if you have good credit and a strong repayment track record. Unfortunately, if you have a history of late payments, they may be more reluctant to offer you a deal. If that's the case, don't despair—you're about to learn a definitively non-Olympian sport: credit card surfing.

Many credit cards, with their insatiable hunger for new customers, offer single-digit introductory "teaser" rates to lure you to sign up. Once the introductory period is up, the rates usually skyrocket to the same old harsh rates you've been paying on your other cards. Credit card companies know, however, that most people are too lazy to switch to a lower-interest card. They count on this complacency, but if you're willing to do a little credit card choreography, you can save hundreds, possibly thousands, of dollars a year.

Simply apply for a card with a low teaser rate (go to www. ramresearch.com for some of the most competitive deals) and then transfer your existing balances to the teaser card. If you are approaching the teaser deadline and you still carry a balance, don't sweat it. Apply for a new teaser card, transfer your balance once again, and cancel the old card. Banks don't monitor these things, so you can keep surfing until your statement reaches the magic zero. On a $10,000 balance, you would save about $1,000 a year in interest—just by doing about five minutes of work. That's a rate even Bill Gates would envy.

LISTEN UP! No-brainer Savings Advice

Did you know a few clicks of your mouse can save you a fortune in credit card interest? There are now low-interest credit cards that you can apply for only through the Web. In the rush to sign up new customers, these sites aggressively offer single-digit rates rarely found in nature. For example, Nextcard (www.nextcard.com) currently offers a Visa with an initial APR as low as 2.9 percent before switching to a still-fantastic 9.9 percent after the introductory period. You can even pay your monthly statements over the computer by linking your checking account to your Nextcard. Even better, transfer all of your other balances to your low-interest Nextcard on-line—no phone calls, no forms to fill out, just a few pecks on the keyboard and cyberspace takes care of the rest.

INCENTIVE PLANS

Every financial guidebook we've come across urges readers to get in on these so-called give back programs—enormously popular programs where credit card issuers reward cardholders with everything from frequent flier miles to gasoline to kitchen appliances. After all, the theory goes, you're getting something for nothing—a true rarity in today's world. However, unless you charge the equivalent of a developing nation's GNP and pay it off at the end of every month, you're paying dearly for those freebies.

Say you belong to a frequent-flier plan that awards a free domestic ticket after 25,000 miles. Usually, that means you have to charge $25,000 worth of stuff before you get a free domestic coach ticket. Now look in your newspaper's travel section and find the most expensive coach ticket between two U.S. cities. We looked recently and found a ticket from New York to Seattle for $500. If it takes you four years to charge that much on your card, watch how quickly that "free ticket" can end up costing you more than a flight on the Concorde.

Airline Tie-in Cards Carry Higher Annual Fees

You now know that there is no reason in the world to pay an annual fee. Even if for some reason you do choose a card with a fee, airline cards almost always carry higher fees. Where regular cards generally charge a membership fee of between $25 and $50 a year, airline cards start at $85 and can climb to as high as $125. After four years you've already paid at least $150 more than you had to for the privilege of earning free miles.

You Lose the Power to Negotiate

It gets worse. Many credit card companies will lower your interest rates if you simply call their customer service department and ask them to. Try that with an airline card and you'll get a lesson in hardball diplomacy. Banks are notoriously inflexible when it comes to airline cards. Once I called Citibank and asked them to waive my $85 annual fee for my American Airlines Visa. I asked nicely. I tried to reason with them. Were they really prepared to lose a customer who paid an average of $2,000 in interest a year over an $85 fee? Apparently they were. I even spoke to a supervisor—no luck. But when I switched my card to a plain vanilla Visa and told the customer service representative I was dissatisfied with the terms of our agreement, I got quite a different reaction. The representative did everything he could to keep me happy short of coming over and cleaning my house. Not only did he waive the fee, but he offered me a 6.9 percent rate for the next six months—a huge difference from the 20.9 percent I was paying. I watched my finance charges plummet from $170 a month to $65. Over five months, those savings alone could pay for a cross-country ticket.

Milk Isn't the Only Thing That Expires

There was a time not so long ago when every mile you earned was yours to keep. Airlines treated miles like a marriage—it was strictly 'til death do you part. Now some airlines have adopted tough "use-it-or-lose-it" policies for their members. Miles not redeemed by a certain date (usually three years from the date credited to your account) simply vanish into thin air. Never to be seen again. Ever.

That's enough to give any miles addict a coronary. We earned those miles through blood, sweat, and tears, and no one's going to take them away from us. We resolve to do anything to cash them in, and in our determination to make the award level in time we can get a little stupid, either by buying things we don't need or taking unnecessary trips. We know more than a few people who've gone on retail binges just to top off their account and collect that free ticket. I once used the fear of expiring miles to rationalize buying a couch before I had the money. I racked up another $1,500 on my credit cards, but, hey—now I could fly to Miami for free!

Before you sign up for these perk programs, it pays to keep in mind the old adage "there's no such thing as a free lunch." Unless your job has a bottomless expense account that flies you to Japan three times a year, it is very hard to win at this game. (If everyone did, do you really think airlines and credit cards would hawk them so tirelessly?) Banks design these programs with only one thing in mind—to get you to spend more money and feed their bottom line. All of the prizes, be they free travel, upgrades, homemade ice cream makers, whatever, are seldom more than distractions designed to blind you from the cold hard math of these programs. When you walk away, you are giving yourself one less motive for using your credit cards. It may be hard at first to reach for the plastic knowing you're getting nothing extra, but that's the point. If you can't quit these programs cold turkey, satisfy your mileage cravings in other, less potentially damaging ways. For example, consider linking your long distance to an incentive program— your jaw might hurt after a while, but at least you won't go broke.

CASH ADVANCES

After you read this section, the next time you need a quick cash infusion, you might find selling an organ in Brazil a more attractive option for raising money. As unreasonable as interest rates on cards can seem, they don't hold a candle to the special treatment banks have set aside for cash borrowers. First, they hit you with a hefty fee for each transaction, usually ranging from 3 percent to 5 percent. On a $1,000 advance, that can cost as much as $50! Then, they slaughter you with unconscionable interest rates that make the standard rates look downright charitable. (By the way, there's never a grace period on cash loans, so interest begins accruing the moment the ATM spits out your money.) And if you think you can get around cash advance rates by using those so-called convenience checks the banks periodically send in the mail, think again. Most banks treat those checks the same as a cash advance. You can also forget about negotiating cash advance rates and fees with your bank—they know they have you.

In a cash crunch you might be able to convince yourself that you can live with those terms. After all, you just need the cash for a few days and you can pay it back as soon as you get the next paycheck. Once again, the banks have thought of a clever way to keep you in hock for a looooong time.

Banks, you see, first apply your payment toward the purchases portion of the balance, which carries a lower interest rate. If you carry a balance, only a small percentage of your payment is applied to the cash advance. Even if you mail a check the next day for the full amount of the advance, the bulk of it will be applied to your purchases, leaving much of the cash advance in place to accrue interest at those horrible rates.

A Cautionary Tale

Lisa didn't have enough money to pay her rent. Her landlord's a real stickler, so rather than be late, Lisa hit the ATM and borrowed a month's rent on her card. For the purposes of this example let's choose an arbitrary amount of $1,400. (Lisa found a "real bargain" in Manhattan.) When her next paycheck came, Lisa immediately sent a $1,400 check to Visa and thought she had washed her hands of the loan.

Lisa was in for a rude awakening, however, when she opened her next statement. Because she carried a high balance, the bank applied $1,100 to the balance, leaving only $300 for the cash advance. She was still responsible for the interest on $1,100 of the cash advance! The next month Lisa scraped together the $1,100 and sent it in, and you can probably guess what happened next. This time only $260 was applied to the cash advance, leaving about $840 collecting interest daily. All told, it took Lisa five months and $150 in interest to pay back an advance she had the money to repay in a week.

The good news is that after you finish this book you'll never be at the mercy of these plastic robber barons. You'll know how to budget your money so you're not forced to make unpleasant choices like Lisa's. But if you do find yourself in a bind, do yourself a favor—beg, steal, or borrow before you turn to your credit card for ready cash.

> **LISTEN UP! No-brainer Savings Advice**
>
> Use the Web to find the best credit card deal for you. Whether you're after low rates, low fees, or a strong affinity card, cardweb.com provides complete surveys of the best cards available in their category. For added convenience, many of the carriers allow you to download an application.

OTHER TIPS

Don't Let Banks Increase Your Limit Without Permission

To the financial experts' old saying "We spend what we earn," I would add "We charge what we can." If you're a responsible payer, banks don't care how much you owe as long as you keep making those interest-soaked minimum payments each month. While you're not looking, many banks will quietly raise your limit until you're a $20,000-a-year assistant with a $15,000 credit limit. That's a recipe for disaster, since balances have this strange tendency to settle at their limits. Avoid this fate by asking your issuer to freeze your limit at its current level. Or, if you want to get really aggressive, slash your limit as you pay off your balance. Keep some room for emergencies, but you'll sleep better knowing that even the worst shopping binge can only do a fraction of the damage of the old days.

Think Twice before Investing in Gold and Platinum

Despite what the credit card companies want you to believe, having a gold or platinum card does not make you more impressive. Nor does it make you part of an exclusive group. I got my first gold card when I was 23 years old and sat in a cubicle three feet away from the copy room. These cards offer few extras you will actually use, and can carry annual fees more than $50 higher than regular cards. Premium cards don't necessarily entitle you to higher credit limits either, which after reading this chapter you know to run like hell from anyway.

To find out if these cards are actually worth it for you, call your issuer and ask for a list of benefits their "elite" program offers. Most of the perks involve travel—car and hotel upgrades are common perks, as is collision insurance on rental cars—so if you spend a lot of time on the road, the higher fee might be worth it. If not, a standard card should be just fine.

Read the Fine Print in Every Month's Statement

We know this can be a little tedious, but if you don't, you risk falling victim to one of the credit card companies' most odious practices. In this perfectly legal scam, companies insert a flier into your statement announcing, in extremely small print, new, higher interest rates. You usually have the option of closing the account and paying off your balance at the old rate, but use the card just once after the notice has been sent (even if you toss it out unread), and the bank (as well as the law) will view that as automatic acceptance of the new terms.

In essence, this means that issuers can arbitrarily change the terms of a previously executed business transaction. Why this is legal we don't understand, but if you just take a few seconds to peer into the envelope each month, you won't ever have to worry that the cashmere sweater you charged last winter at 15 percent will be sitting in summer storage at 21 percent.

Separate Work from Play

When I first got my expense account I felt like the adult world had finally asked me to become a member. I quickly proved, however, that when it came to acting responsibly, I had a lot of growing up to do. I wined and dined business contacts, plunked down $150 a shot for house seats to the hottest Broadway shows, and racked up huge bills staying at hotels I could never afford on my own. Then, six weeks later when my company reimbursed me with a check that sometimes totaled thousands of dollars, I treated it as a windfall—*some* of the money went to paying back the credit card, but not before I skimmed some off the top for personal stuff. Those checks made it very easy to fool myself into thinking I had extra money to burn.

The easiest way to sidestep this danger is to ask your boss for a corporate credit card. With a corporate card, expenses are billed directly to your employer. There are no weekly expense reports, no reimbursement checks, and, since the money never passes through your hands for even a second, no temptation. If your company doesn't offer these cards, you can still keep your personal expenses separate from your business ones. Simply get a card and use it exclusively for business expenses. Keep it in a special place in your wallet away from your other cards, and apply for a low credit limit that gives you enough room to charge expenses for one reimbursement cycle. Since you will be paying this card off every month, you don't care about the interest rate. Just make sure it has a reasonable grace period and no annual fee, and you'll avoid having one of the best perks of any job become a costly contributor to your financial mess.

If You're Really In over Your Head . . .

Okay . . . so you're at the end of this chapter. You've clipped all unnecessary cards, jousted with the nice customer service lady in Sioux Falls, and ditched your incentive programs, but it still looks like it'll take a case of divine intervention to get you back on your feet. You do have another option before calling the bankruptcy lawyer. Consider using a nonprofit debt-counseling agency such as Consumer Credit Counseling Service (800-278-8811) or Budget and Credit Counseling Services (212-675-5070). If you do use their services, it may be noted on your credit report, so ask first. If you're uncomfortable discussing your financial situation with a stranger, try myvesta.org, an on-line service that can broker a repayment plan acceptable to both you and your creditors. Organizations like these have an excellent track record negotiating lower interest rates and monthly payments and, best of all, you will be charged based on your ability to pay. Even if you can't afford to pay anything, they won't turn you away.

CHEAT SHEET

Imagine a life free from minimum payments, 18.9 percent interest, and annoying phone calls from American Express. Conquer your plastic demons and you will be well on your road to debt-free bliss.

- *Negotiate a lower interest rate.* It's your right as an American to have a reasonable APR. Call your card issuer and ask for one. If they refuse, take your business (and your balance) elsewhere.
- *Learn to credit card surf.* You can substantially lower your interest rates by taking advantage of introductory teaser rates that many cards offer. Just be sure to switch cards again before the rate increases.
- *There's no such thing as a free ticket.* Unless you pay your bill in full every month, credit card "freebies" are costing you a bundle. Take a moment and calculate what you're getting back in exchange for paying higher fees and interest.
- *Cash advances: an offer you can refuse.* Even the Godfather offers better terms for borrowing money than a credit card. Unless it's an absolute emergency, *never* take out a cash advance.
- *Keep a separate card for business expenses.* If you lay out

your own money for business expenses, you should know
exactly what part of your debt is business-related and what
part is personal. Keeping a separate card for business will
encourage you to use company reimbursement checks solely
for the business credit card.

6

Everything You Always Wanted to Know About Banking but Feared Being Bored out of Your Skull

We all remember our first bank account. For many of us, it was a passbook savings account where we deposited the $50 Grandma sent to us every year on our birthday. The account earned maybe 3 percent interest, and we stuck the passbook in the toy chest and promptly forgot about it. As a teenager, we graduated to a checking account and learned bad habits like writing checks for $1.92 for a bag of Chee-tos at the convenience store.

Most of us don't give our bank a second thought—it's nothing more than a checking account and an ATM card. Banks are all the same, right? Wrong.

In the past few years, banks have become much more aggressive in finding ways to squeeze cash out of their customers. The result? We're stuck with fees that can approach $10 a month for the privilege of holding your money interest-free. Bounced check fees can run as high as $30 (it costs a bank less than $1 to process a returned check). And the most recent irritating "innovation"? You get stuck with an access fee every time you use some other bank's ATM.

Over time, these fees can add up to a serious chunk of change. One year I spent over $400 (more than two months of credit card payments!) on bank fees. Of course most of these were completely avoidable. What's the solution? Well, you could revolt and hide your cash in a cannister under your bed. Or you can get smart. We recommend the latter.

WHAT'S YOUR BANKING IQ?

Here's your chance just to see much banking guidance you need. It's easy! No number 2 pencils necessary! Just read the following ten statements and write in your answer. After calculating your banking IQ, you'll know just how closely you'll need to pay attention to the rest of this chapter.

1 = "That's totally me."
3 = "I do that sometimes."
5 = "You must mean somebody else."

____ I write more than eight checks a month.
____ I use the ATM at least twice a week.
____ I generally take out $20–$40 every time I go to the ATM.
____ I almost never open my bank statement.
____ Checking accounts are all the same, right?
____ "Minimum balance" is something you need after drinking too much.
____ I always use that ATM in the convenience store instead of my bank ATM because it's just so *convenient.*
____ I always know *about* how much money I have in my account.
____ I can't use a credit union because it's only for people in unions.
____ I balanced my checkbook . . . once.

Okay, it's time to tabulate your score. Drumroll please.

If you scored between 35 and 50 points, you're a *banking dream*. You probably already have all the good habits that help you avoid usurious bank fees, ATM charges, and bounced-check penalties. Congratulations! You now have our permission to snicker at the less fortunate *banking duds*.

If you're like most people—and let's face it, who isn't like "most people"—then you probably scored between 15 and 35. This is nothing to be ashamed of. After reading this chapter, you'll be able to avoid even the sneakiest of the banks' sneaky tricks. You'll find out all the scintillating secrets behind those mysterious "account fees" on your monthly statement.

If you scored between 10 and 15 (God help the person who scored 10), then you're a *banking dud*. This "dud" is the type of person who throws away his or her bank statement, keeps an average balance of $12.97, and uses the ATM twice a day to withdraw $10. Don't get freaked out if you fall into this unfortunate category. Lots of smart, successful people used to be banking duds (in fact, two of them are writing a book about it). However, you'll need to pay really close attention to this chapter.

One of These Things Is Just Like the Other: Banks, Savings and Loans, and Credit Unions

This is one of life's less interesting, but eternal, questions: what exactly is the difference between a bank, savings and loan, and credit union? Answer: not much. (Now don't you feel better?) For someone seeking basic financial services—ATM usage, checking, etc.—there's really no functional difference between these institutions. Most of the time credit unions are cheaper than many banks, because a credit union is generally formed by, and limited to, a specific profession or group. (We'll talk more about this later.)

Picking the Bank That's Right for You

The first time I had to select a bank was during my freshman year in college. I picked my new bank based on the following criteria:

- Location
- Cool logo design
- Availability of checks customized with cute woodland creatures

The first reason was pretty practical. The second and third reasons I'll attribute to youthful stupidity. At the age of eighteen, I didn't quite get the comic irony of a check illustrated with frolicking deer and dewy pine trees stamped "Insufficient Funds" in frightening red ink. Now I'm older and much wiser, my checks are the basic blue, and I've managed to find an account that meets my needs without gouging me with fees.

Here are some basic criteria you can use to pick the bank, savings and loan, or credit union that's right for you. (We'll just refer to these institutions collectively as "banks" from now on.)

Convenient ATM Locations

If one-third of your life is spent sleeping and one-third is spent working, where do you spend the other one-third? The ATM. Location should be a key consideration when choosing a bank.

Sure, there are ATMs *everywhere* now—from grocery stores to airports to office buildings. But it's a sucker's paradise, because most of these "convenient" locations come with a price. These independent ATMs generally charge between $1 or $2 *plus* whatever your bank charges you for using another ATM.

Before you choose a bank, scout around your home or office to check if there are nearby ATM locations. Having your bank's ATM nearby prevents you from rationalizing the extra buck you'll spend using someone else's ATM. If you're traveling, most banks have an

800 number you can call to find a local bank that offers free or lower-fee ATM services.

Small Is Beautiful: Community Banks

As a big-city resident, my old bank is one of those billion dollar behemoths with branch offices sandwiched between every Starbucks and Gap. Unfortunately, it's also the kind of place where you're just an eleven-digit number rather than a customer. Every time I called with a problem, I got one of those elaborate electronic answering systems that did everything except answer my questions. After twenty minutes of punching through various options, I'd reach a dead end and an electronic voice would give a terse "good-bye" before hanging up on me. It was infuriating. Speaking to a *real-live human being* just became impossible.

As an alternative, you might consider choosing a smaller bank. (This is what I did.) Lots of smaller banks try to focus on customer service as a way of competing with the giants. These smaller banks also offer some of the most competitive checking fees around (but we'll discuss that more in a bit). Small bank managers are also frequently more lenient when it comes to negotiating lower returned-check charges and other fees. If you're the kind of bank customer who needs a lot of hand-holding, a small bank is an option worth considering.

Use the Internet for Something Other Than E-mail and Finding Naked Pictures of Dr. Laura: Welcome to Internet Banking

On the opposite end of the banking spectrum is the kind of financial institution perfect for low-maintainance technophiles whose idea of good customer service is an automated E-mail. If you're the kind of self-reliant bank customer who never wants to walk into another branch office again, an Internet bank might be the place for you. Now don't get this confused with electronic or on-line banking—this is a service that a lot of traditional banks offer. An

Internet bank is a bank that exists solely in cyberspace. No branches. No teller windows. No scratchy pens with chains attached.

The upside: Internet banks have really low operating costs so they frequently offer some of the lowest fees around. Most of your checks are handled electronically so checking fees are generally incredibly low. Also, in an effort to attract customers, some of the Internet banks offer substantially higher interest rates on savings accounts, certificates of deposit, and money-market accounts.

Of course there are drawbacks—you have to use other banks' ATMs (although many Internet banks offer monthly credits to cover these charges), you have to mail in paper deposits, and there's no branch office to go to if you ever quickly need a cashier's check, money order, or to complain to someone in person.

If you're looking for some of the cheapest fees around and don't mind logging on rather than walking in, an Internet bank may be worth a try.

Two of our favorite Internet banks are etradebank.com and Wingspan.com. These are full-service financial institutions that offer everything a traditional bank offers (except a building)—checking, money-market accounts, CDs, savings accounts, brokerage services, insurance, mortgage lending, car loans, and credit cards. Both E*TRADE Bank and Wingspan offer some serious perks, including savings rates in the top 1 percent nationally and money-market yields that are double the national average. And as I write this, E*TRADE Bank offers *free, unlimited* electronic checking—plus free paper checks. Another benefit: both of these banks balance your checkbook *automatically*.

Unfortunately the good times probably won't last forever, but right now these Internet banks offer great deals for the tech-savvy customer.

Get Credit Where Credit Is Due: Credit Unions

A credit union is a lower cost alternative to a lot of full-service banks. These types of financial institutions generally offer better rates on loans and cheaper fees for checking accounts. (Lots of credit unions even offer no-fee checking and waive minimum balance requirements.) If you're eligible, then a credit union is a good, low-cost alternative to a bank.

The drawbacks? Credit unions generally don't offer the broad range of services that a regular bank does. So if you're looking for a financial institution with electronic banking, brokerage services, or financial advising, then a credit union is probably not for you. Also, lots of credit unions don't have their own ATMs (again with the ATMs!), so many times you'll be forced to eat fees at other banks' electronic tellers.

If you work for the government, a large corporation, or in the public sector in a school or a hospital, then you're probably eligible for a credit union in your area. Also, you should find out if anyone in your immediate family banks at a credit union. Lots of credit unions allow family members to take advantage of the same low-cost services.

You can find a complete list of U.S. credit unions on-line at www.creditunionsonline.com. This is a great resource—you can search alphabetically or by state to find the eligibility requirements for credit unions in your area.

WELCOME TO YOUR CHECKING ACCOUNT

Food, water, shelter, and a checking account—this basic financial service has become one of the necessities of everyday living. Unfortunately, the banks know this, and they're finding new and interesting ways to charge us more and more for this "convenience" (i.e., necessity). Monthly charges can range from $5 to $15 just for holding your money. Lots of banks also limit the number of checks you can write each month (generally 5–10). You may get charged up to *40 cents* for each check you write above this limit.

At most banks, the only way to avoid these exorbitant checking account fees is to maintain a "minimum balance"—this is the amount of money you need to keep in your banking account to qualify for free or low-cost checking. At some banks this minimum balance can be as low as $500. But for many of us, it's likely going to be $1,000 or more.

This "minimum balance" should be a key criterion when you're on the lookout for cheap banking. It's good to ask friends or do a little research on-line to find a bank that's willing to cut costs. Complete the process with a couple of phone calls to the banks you're considering. This should determine who offers the best deal.

Hey You! FEES!

Yes, I too know the sting of outrageous bank charges. Before I started down the road to debt-free living, I routinely tossed my bank statements in the drawer without even looking at them. Little did I know I was paying up to *thirty bucks* a month in stupid charges. Plus, this money was being deducted from my account automatically, so I never even noticed it.

Unbeknownst to yours truly, I was spending almost $250 a year on banking charges I didn't even realize existed. Once I made this simple discovery, I quickly remedied the situation by finding a lower-cost alternative and watching my money management habits.

Here's an example of what I spent in one month on needless, useless checking and ATM fees before I learned my lesson.

FINDING THE BEST CHECKING ACCOUNT FOR YOU

There are some other things you should consider when you start looking for the perfect checking account. How do you use this account? What's the minimum balance requirement? Does using "direct deposit" lower my fees? You'll need to ask these questions and much, much more to get the best deal.

Karl's Monthly Fee Summary

Total of twenty transactions for this statement period.

Five checks paid $2.50
Four in-bank ATM withdrawals $2.00
Yep, since my account only allowed me to perform ten transactions (this means checks and ATM withdrawals) a month for free, I got charged 50 cents for every check I wrote over this limit. Because of a few extra payments—like my quarterly car insurance—I got stuck with these charges.

Four nonbank ATM withdrawals $4.00
Every time I used an out-of-network ATM, my bank charged me a buck. Of course, this didn't count the $1–2 transaction fee that the out-of-network ATM charged as well.

One pre-authorized debits $0.50
Since I went over my ten-transaction limit, my bank also charged me for my student loan payment being automatically debited from my account. Nice.

Point-of-sale transactions $0.50
You know those "handy" debit cards. This is listed as a "point-of-sale transaction." I got charged for this too.

Monthly maintenance $9.50
9.50!!! This is my favorite charge. After billing me $9.50 for a few checks and my ATM usage, they charge me another $9.50 just for holding my money—interest free.

Total $19.00
After reviewing several bank statements, this was a pretty typical monthly charge. Basically, it was an idiot tax—because I was too dumb to open my monthly statement and realize I was being taken for a ride.

Unlike spandex or KISS reunion concert tour T-shirts, checking accounts are not one-size-fits-all products. Different types of people have different requirements. You should try to find an account that meets your needs.

Are you a rough-and-tumble, six- or seven-checks-a-month kind of person? You write a fixed number of checks each month. One for the rent. One for your car payment. Then a couple more for your electric and phone bill. This type of person should consider a basic checking account. These accounts charge you a low fee in exchange for limiting the number of checks you write each month and by limiting the number of times you can use the ATM.

If you get this type of account, then it's important to closely monitor the number of transactions you are making each month. Remember: it's not just checks they're counting, but the number of ATM withdrawals you're making as well.

Are you a banking primadonna who writes 10+ checks a month? If you're still writing checks for $7.13 at the grocery store, then it's time to have your head examined. You're probably paying fees up the wazoo for your wasteful ways. As a rule, you should try to keep your check writing to a minimum. There are several ways to do this, such as signing up for direct payment for standard monthly expenses, which we'll discuss a little later. However, if you need full-service checking rather than a basic or "lifeline" account, it's best to bite the bullet and maintain the minimum balance. There are some clever ways to do this, all of which I'll tell you about right now.

PISS OFF, CITIBANK!! HOW TO AVOID THOSE ANNOYING FEES

Okay, now that you know everything about these dreaded *fees*, it's time to learn how to avoid them. Don't worry, it's not hard. You'll be an expert in no time.

- *Learn the minimum balancing act.* "Minimum balance" sounds easy, right? But like everything else, banks have a way of making the simplest concepts incredibly difficult. It's important to remember when you're choosing a bank to ask how the bank calculates your account's minimum balance. Some banks require you to have a minimum balance—say of $500—every single day of the statement period. This means if your balance ends only $0.01 under for one day, you get stuck with an entire month's fees.

  Try to find a bank that calculates the minimum balance using the "average daily balance method." Here the bank simply averages your balance over the length of your statement cycle. So if you have $250 one day and then $750 the next, it averages out and you're fine. This ensures that if you go a little under for one day, then you're not going to get completely screwed for the entire month.

- *Use direct deposit.* Most employers offer a super-easy option called "direct deposit." So instead of forgeting to deposit your paycheck again . . . and again . . . and again, the money will be automatically deposited into your checking accounts. What makes this even better? Many banks will waive some of the monthly fees and minimum balance requirements if you sign up for direct deposit. It's easy to take advantage of this—just ask your human resource representative, office manager, or payroll administrator.

- *Find a bank that lets you combine accounts to meet the minimum balance.* You know all that money you're stashing away in your savings account, money market account, or certificates of deposit (CDs)? Huh?! Okay, maybe you don't have any money in these accounts, but now you have another good reason to start. Some banks let you "link" your various accounts to meet the minimum balance requirements. For example, say your bank has a $1,000 minimum balance. If you stash $1,000 in a *combination* of accounts—like a savings account, CDs, money market, whatever—then this qualifies as your minimum balance and you get free or low-cost checking! (Note: The minimum balance may be higher when you link accounts. Some banks require a minimum balance that's double the checking minimum balance when you combine funds.)

See, sometimes life *is* fair. Now you have an incentive to save and avoid those fees at the same time.

- *Consider electronic or on-line banking.* Lots of big banks are aggressively pushing electronic or on-line banking as the latest, greatest banking convenience. Since banks have an interest in getting consumers to adopt this technology (because it cuts down on paperwork and makes their operations more profitable), it's also one of the cheapest ways to do your banking. (Note: this is different from Internet banks, which are banks that exist solely in cyberspace.)

There are differences between "electronic" and on-line banking. "Electronic banking" usually means you have to get special software for your computer and connect to the bank at a specific number. "On-line banking" means you conduct all of your business on a secured Web page. More than likely, you'll see banks move toward on-line banking because it's easier to implement and more convenient for consumers.

Electronic and on-line banking is incredibly convenient. Instead of writing a check each month, searching for a stamp, and then forgetting to stick it in the mail (and sending it two weeks late), you can simply log on, enter the account number of the person or company you're paying, and the amount you owe, then *voilà*! The money is either electronically transferred or the bank sends out a printed check. Cool, huh?

Another great thing about this type of banking is that all your records are stored in one place. If you forgot how much you sent the phone company last month, you can log on to your computer and find the record. It's also a good way to manage money *between* accounts, so if you're running a little short for the month you can transfer money from a savings account into your checking. You can also have fixed monthly payments, like loans, paid automatically every month on the same date.

Within five years, most consumer banking will be conducted electronically. It saves the banks money, and most people find it a lot more convenient than writing paper checks. Don't you want to be a tech-savvy, "early adopter"? Here's your chance to get a head start on your friends and neighbors.

- *Beware of false prophets! . . . and overdraft protection.* Ah, the dreaded bounced check. Insufficient funds. The big rubber return-to-sender. It's one of life's little humiliations. You get that ominous, computerized notice in the mail that accuses you of being a deadbeat. Or even worse, someone you know gently reminds you, *"Remember that check you wrote me . . . ?"* It's embarrassing and shows the world how irresponsible you are.

  To make it even worse, banks charge upward of $20 each time one of your checks gets dinged for insufficient funds. So if you accidently write an entire series of checks against an empty account, you get charged for each one. And then you're *really* in the hole.

  Most banks offer some form of "overdraft protection" to protect your fragile ego from these painful moments. As a book dedicated to getting you out of debt, we're somewhat reluctant to recommend signing up for this service. Why? Overdraft protection is a high-interest loan (interest rates are generally comparable to a credit card) that covers you when you don't have the money in your account to cover a check. Sounds great, right?

  If you use it wisely, overdraft protection can save you money on stupid insufficient funds charges. At the same time, lots of people (I used to do this) use the overdraft protection as a de facto credit card—paying interest month after month while spending more and more and getting deeper and deeper in debt.

Check This!

Ray is a typically ambitious, professional 25-year-old—single, unencumbered, and just starting to wise up. He signed up for a checking account when he moved to Arizona and hadn't thought a lot about it since. "I just randomly selected my bank. I didn't even know there were different types of checking accounts." Ironically, Ray worked as a news producer covering consumer stories. "I'd produced dozens of stories on getting the best deal on a car or a home loan—whatever. It's embarrassing that I never realized I was getting destroyed each month with checking fees." He laughed. "I could've done a story on myself."

Ray never really paid any attention to his bank statements. "It's the last thing you want to look at when you get home from work." One day Ray received a bounced-check notice from the bank. He recalled, "I thought I had just enough money to cover the check. But I never considered my monthly banking charges." He finally opened his statement (he was used to tossing them in the drawer unopened), and noticed almost $30 in bank fees. "Between the ATM charges, the check fees, and the 'account maintenance' charge, I was being eaten alive."

He analyzed his banking habits. "I wrote fourteen or fifteen checks a month and used the ATM all the time. I didn't even know there was such thing as a minimum balance." Because Ray had signed up for the basic or "lifeline" checking, he was being charged for everything after the tenth transaction. Ray decided to switch from a "lifeline" checking account to a regular one with a minimum balance option. "Since I had some money in savings at another bank, I decided to consolidate my accounts." He explained, "I put my savings into a money-market account (the minimum was $2,500) at the same bank as my checking account. This way I received free checking." Ray added, "Plus, the money market account is earning a higher interest rate than my old savings account."

How does this happen? Ignorantly, I assumed that when I made my next deposit, the amount charged to my overdraft protection would automatically get paid off. Wrong. You have to specifically write a check (or transfer money at the ATM) to the overdraft protection account. Much to my dismay, I was charged a monthly minimum fee (again like a credit card) for the interest accruing in my overdraft protection account. I never paid off the principal, so the next time I was short on cash my overdraft protection account got charged again. Then I owed even more money. Plus, I could access the overdraft account from the ATM. So if I was short on cash—well, I could withdraw money directly from the overdraft protection for that too! This went on and on and on . . . until I had charged so much in my overdraft protection account I couldn't begin to pay it off. It's called a slippery slope, folks.

Gentle reader, learn from my mistakes. If you're going to get overdraft protection, be very, very, very careful. Sometimes the solution can be worse than the problem.

ATM Means "Automatically Takes Your Money"

Let's not kid ourselves. The ATM is one of the great modern conveniences of our time. For most people in their twenties, we can't even *imagine* a world without them. *What did people do? Go to the bank and wait in line to withdraw $40? Gasp!* There was actually a time when people were *afraid* to use an ATM, and the banks made them free to encourage people to use them. Now they've got us all hooked on this convenience. Unfortunately, this convenience comes with a rather inconvenient cost.

Most ATMs charge some kind of fee, usually between $1 and $2. If you use the machine a few times each week, you could be spending more than fifty bucks a month on unnecessary charges. Plus, if you use an ATM that's not owned by your bank, you can end up getting charged *twice*. Your bank charges you for using another ATM, and then the ATM owner charges you a usage fee. This can be an expensive proposition, sometimes upward of three bucks.

In chapter 2 you figured out where all your money is going. Now you know what you can realistically budget each week for incidental expenses. You should use this information to help control your ATM usage. Instead of stopping by the ATM every time you need money, take out a fixed amount at the beginning of every week. This helps you keep closer tabs on your spending habits and prevents you from going back and forth to the ATM, racking up needless usage fees. If you go to the ATM every Sunday for your week's cash, and you're broke by Thursday—you know you're doing something wrong.

I Was a Twentysomething ATM Addict

"I'd go at least once every other day, and on the weekends I might go twice in the same day." Hannah looks back ruefully at this painful time, "It was like I was addicted to the ATM." Hannah, a 23-year-old development associate for a nonprofit agency in Atlanta, racked up outrageous ATM fees without even noticing it. "I thought I was being financially responsible for only taking out $20 or $30 at a time from the ATM. Meanwhile I was probably spending $350 a year on ATM charges."

Hannah made a classic bad money error—having less money in your pocket to spend doesn't necessarily mean you'll spend less. "I thought if I only took out $20 then I would only spend $20. Instead I just ended up going back to the ATM incessantly. It was stupid." Hannah analyzed her expenses and decided she could cover all her food, incidental, and entertainment expenses by withdrawing $150 every Monday. "It seemed weird to be taking out so much money, but it really helped me balance my budget. I knew exactly how much I had to spend for the week, so it helped me allocate my money. If I didn't make the money last, it was peanut butter and jelly until next Monday. Three days of that and I never ran out of money again."

Okay, okay . . . we know you're tired of hearing about maintaining a minimum balance. Honestly, though, it's one of the best ways to control those stupid bank charges. Find out what the rules are with your account. A basic "lifeline" checking account generally gives you a fixed number of free transactions and then charges you $0.50 to $1 for everything over that—including ATM charges. A regular checking account may allow you to use the ATM for free as long as you maintain a minimum balance. If your account drops below this minimum, you could get slapped with a fee every time you write a check or use the ATM. The most important thing is just to understand the rules of your particular account.

But He/She Loves Me! Thinking Twice Before Getting a Joint Checking Account

Okay, here's where everything starts to get tricky. Boy meets girl. Or boy meets boy. Or girl meets girl. The two smitten young lovers decide that they want to share everything—including that most serious of commitments, a joint checking account. This is an account where two people have access to the account—for deposits, check writing, ATM withdrawals, and whatever.

We all know people who think less about moving in with someone than they do about giving that special someone access to their hard-earned cash. If you're married, everything is obviously much more simple because there are laws that govern who gets what in the event things don't work out. If you're not married, things start to get complicated if "I love you" turns to "take your crap and your ugly face and get out."

There are two types of joint accounts:

Joint convenience account: This account gives two people access to the same account for all the normal banking services. If one of the partners dies, it doesn't guarantee the other one the right to inherit the money in the account.

Joint account with the right of survivorship: This type of account offers more legal protection for the surviving partner. So if one of the partners checks out prematurely, the joint account holder inherits the money in the account.

Bob and Colleen

Married for about two years, Bob and Colleen, both 27-year-old graphic designers, decided to make the final, ultimate commitment. "In some ways it was the hardest decision to make," Colleen recalls. "Love is blind, but money . . . is *money*." Bob and Colleen decided to close their personal accounts and open a joint account. Bob offers, "We were trying to save money to buy a house, so it just seemed to make more sense to keep our money together where we could track each other's spending." They set up the account at the same bank as a shared mutual savings account, so they could "link" the accounts, maintain the minimum balance, and qualify for free checking.

So far the solution seems to be working. "I definitely think twice about writing a check or making a withdrawal, because I don't want Bob to go to the ATM for a withdrawal and be left without any money." To manage their expenses they got an erasable board in their kitchen. Whenever they take money out of the account, deposit a paycheck, or write a check, they write it on the board. "It makes keeping track of our finances really easy," Bob says. "We know exactly how much money we can put into savings at the end of the month. It makes balancing the checkbook at the end of the month a breeze."

For personal expenses, they collectively withdraw and split $200 at the beginning of each week. Colleen says, "This prevents us from going to the ATM and forgetting about the withdrawal." This money management system has really helped their savings account. "We're already starting to look at houses."

A joint account can be an incredible convenience if you're living with someone and have lots of mutual expenses for things like rent, utilities, and groceries. But it can also be a real mood killer if your beloved drains the account buying expensive dinners and fancy makeup for his other girlfriend.

Here's how two couples we know solved the joint checking account dilemma:

Joe and Rich

"After we moved in together, this just seemed like the next logical step," Joe explained one afternoon. This gay couple, both twenty-eight, decided they needed a joint account to cover their mutual expenses after moving in together. "We made a list of all the expenses we share—rent, telephone, cable, groceries—and decided how much each of us should contribute each month." Since Joe is a lawyer and Rich works for a nonprofit organization, Joe decided to contribute more. Joe laughs. "I felt it's only fair since he's trying to save the world while I'm busy suing it."

Unlike Bob and Colleen, they both kept personal accounts for their incidental expenses and other expenditures. After depositing the agreed-upon amount into the joint account, they put the rest of their paychecks in their own individual accounts. "Joe doesn't need to be accountable to me for everything he spends money on," Rich says. "I think it's easier on the relationship that way."

CHEAT SHEET

- *It's important to find a bank that works for you.* You should consider the bank's location, your proximity to the bank's ATMs, and a checking account that fits your needs and lifestyle. If you're a high maintenance person, maybe you should consider a community bank. If you're low maintenance, an

Internet bank might be the place for you. Regardless, just make sure you're not getting ripped off with exorbitant account fees.

- *Watch those checking account and ATM fees.* Make sure you're not getting charged a bundle for these basic services. Find out if your checking account has a maximum number of transactions per month before you get charged. Also, try to limit your number of ATM visits and only use your bank's own ATMs. This will keep those fees from piling up.
- *Maintain a minimum balance.* You should "link" your savings account to your checking account to ensure a "minimum" balance. At most banks, this qualifies you for free or low-cost checking services.
- *Make a plan before getting a joint checking account.* Make sure you and your partner have a plan to manage a joint checking account. Sharing an account can be a disaster if the money is not managed carefully.

7

Three Things You Can't Avoid: Death, Taxes, and Cher

We've all heard the saying "the only thing certain in life is death and taxes." While advances in science may make the former obsolete (Cher, for one, seems determined to try), taxes are forever.

Contrary to what you've been led to believe, the IRS is not the enemy. Taxes aren't a bad thing. We can thank Uncle Sam for our freeways, schools, and parks. But you shouldn't pay more than your fair share. Lots of people give thousands of extra dollars to the government because they're too lazy or intimidated to learn the basics of taxes.

With combined federal, state, and local taxes often gobbling up to 50 percent of your income, taxes are a huge and inevitable expense. With FICA, disability, and unemployment nibbling at your paycheck fifty-two weeks a year, no one could blame you for wondering sometimes why you work at all. But buried in your return may be a treasure trove of unknown exemptions, deductions, and write-offs just waiting to be discovered.

This chapter will show you how to keep more of your hard-earned money for yourself, avoid interests and penalties, and ward off the dreaded audit. For all the bad press the IRS gets, if you play by the rules, it can be an integral part of your debt-reduction plan.

In fact, maximizing your refund legally is possibly the easiest way to minimize your debt. You have to pay taxes each year anyway—why not get back every last dollar the government says you're entitled to?

Keep in mind, however, that at last count the U.S. tax code has over 6,000,000 words in it—this chapter has 10,567. We can't possibly hit every tax-saving strategy nor tackle every exception or exclusion that may apply to you, so we've stuck to issues of particular interest to taxpayers under 30. Your own circumstances may require more detail than we can offer here.

SHOULD I DO MY OWN TAXES?

Maybe. You need to assess your own tax IQ (not to mention patience) before deciding which way will save you more money. If you're not yet making the big bucks, a standard deduction and a 1040EZ form might be all you need to minimize your tax bill. However, as your income situation changes, you may miss a few deductions and end up by writing a bigger check April 15th. In those cases, scrimping on the CPA's fee is just foolish.

For most people, we recommend using a tax preparer once or twice as a learning experience before taking a stab at it yourself. Most people in their twenties simply don't have the experience to maximize their tax savings. Did you know that you often can deduct interest from student loans under five years old? We didn't.

The first time I used an accountant, he asked me questions I had no idea were relevant to my income taxes. He found money in places I would have never thought to look and gave me suggestions to increase my deductions in the future. The refund I got after using a professional was far larger than anything I could have come up with on my own. And best of all, after one meeting with him, I knew what to itemize the next year.

Hiring a tax preparer doesn't mean you can kick back and wait for your fat refund check to arrive in the mail. Your accountant doesn't have an all-knowing magic wand that will get you the money you deserve. The accountant is at his busiest between January and April 15th. Those three and a half months may account for a major chunk of his income for the year. Consequently, any preparation you do in advance of your meeting will give him more time to work his CPA magic. Follow the steps below to ensure the best service possible.

Find the right preparer. Give identical W-2's to two different preparers and you might be surprised at the differences in each return. One magazine did just that, and the two accountants returned with a refund difference of $3000. Since there is no organization or guidebook that evaluates a preparer's competence, personal references are by far your best bet in finding a good tax preparer. Ask trusted friends and family for recommendations, and give special weight to any recommendation from someone in your profession.

You should also ask the prospective preparer if he is willing to provide additional client references. If he is reluctant, move on. A good accountant has nothing to hide. Ask what percentage of his clients get audited. If the percentage sounds high to you, the IRS may target him as an overaggressive preparer. Stay away. (See "How to Avoid an Audit.")

LISTEN UP! No-brainer Savings Advice

Try to find a prepararer who worked at the IRS. Just as former prosecutors often make the best defense lawyers, these guys have special knowledge picked up behind enemy lines. That can go a long way in helping you prepare an audit-proof return.

Get your paperwork in order. Your tax preparer is not your mother. He is not hired to organize the shoebox of receipts and forms you thrust in his arms before you go out to play with your friends. The more organized you are beforehand, the less time your preparer will need to do your taxes and the less he will charge you. Even if you do your own taxes, keeping your records in order can only help you get more money back.

Here are the most common records you should have before tackling your taxes, although your own situation may require additional documentation:

- *Last year's tax returns.*
- *W-2 forms.* (Make sure you have a W-2 form from every employer. If you changed jobs and moved in the same calendar year, be sure to notify your old employer of your new address. Otherwise, your W-2 may get sent to the old address.)
- *Any tax documents you receive.* These include 1099 forms, interest or dividend statements, etc.
- *Bank account earning statements.* We don't know anyone with a savings account, but if you do have one, get a statement from the bank that lists any gains from interest. Same goes for other bank accounts such as CDs, interest-bearing checking, etc.
- *All eligible receipts.* Don't rely on memory to remember that deductible meal you had last July or that emergency trip to the podiatrist. Gather all business-related or medical receipts together and break them down into categories. If you haven't been all that diligent in saving the receipts, fear not. You can review last year's credit card statements and checking account statements to jog your memory of eligible expenses. (It also provides a great aerial view of your spending habits.) Contact the merchant and ask for a copy of the receipt. If he is unwilling to provide one, try to get a copy from your card issuer. It may take some begging and pleading, but you can get duplicates of the missing receipts from the credit card company. All card issuers keep the original signed receipt on electronic file in the event of a dispute.

    If you need just a few receipts, most companies will happily send you a copy. If, on the other hand, you've saved nothing and are now in a panic over the money you're going to lose, you still have options. Review your monthly statements and use the listings of your charges to tabulate your deductions. In the event you're audited, you'll have to produce the real receipts, but a desperate letter to your card issuer explaining your situation should persuade them to send you copies.

- *Expense diaries.* Does your job require you to keep up with what's going on in the world? If so, you can probably deduct all magazines, newspapers, etc.—heck, even your cable bill—if you can prove that they are necessary for work. Think outside the box on this one. Very few of us leave our jobs behind when we walk out the door at 5:00. Keeping detailed logs of how often you use personal assets such as your car or computer for business will help you determine the correct deduction.

THE CASE OF THE VANISHING PAYCHECK

At one time or another you probably found yourself staring at your paycheck and thinking "How can I *not* be in debt with all these taxes?" You can fantasize all you like, but you can't beat the system. Leona Helmsley tried, and look what happened to her. And with more of your money going toward taxes each year (see box), relief is nowhere in sight.

Understanding what all those numbers mean, which ones you can change, and which ones you can't is the first step to reducing your tax burden. On the next page is a sample pay stub that probably looks something like your own. Take a look at the descriptions below to learn exactly why your paycheck shrinks like a favorite sweater accidentally tossed in the dryer.

- *Gross pay:* The earnings you may in fact deserve but will never see. (See Helmsley, Leona.)

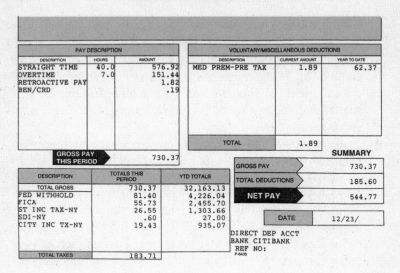

PAY DESCRIPTION			VOLUNTARY/MISCELLANEOUS DEDUCTIONS		
DESCRIPTION	HOURS	AMOUNT	DESCRIPTION	CURRENT AMOUNT	YEAR TO DATE
STRAIGHT TIME	40.0	576.92	MED PREM-PRE TAX	1.89	62.37
OVERTIME	7.0	151.44			
RETROACTIVE PAY		1.82			
BEN/CRD		.19			
			TOTAL	1.89	

GROSS PAY THIS PERIOD	730.37

DESCRIPTION	TOTALS THIS PERIOD	YTD TOTALS
TOTAL GROSS	730.37	32,163.13
FED WITHHOLD	81.40	4,226.04
FICA	55.73	2,455.70
ST INC TAX-NY	26.55	1,303.66
SDI-NY	.60	27.00
CITY INC TX-NY	19.43	935.07
TOTAL TAXES	183.71	

SUMMARY

GROSS PAY	730.37
TOTAL DEDUCTIONS	185.60
NET PAY	544.77
DATE	12/23/

DIRECT DEP ACCT
BANK CITIBANK
REF NO:
P-6435

- *Federal withholding:* Each pay period the federal government takes a percentage of your salary based on an estimate of what your yearly income will be. The percentage is determined by the number of exemptions you claim and your actual salary. Because the United States works on a progressive, or graduated, tax system, the percentage of tax you pay increases as your income rises. The federal government allows you to reduce total taxable income (or AGI, adjusted gross income) through a vast number of deductions and credits.
- *FICA:* No, not a plant, but shorthand for the Federal Income Contributions Act. You know it as social security. Originally started in the thirties as a retirement fund, social security was a miniscule deduction when it was first implemented. Now, however, it swallows a hefty 7.65 percent of your paycheck, up to a maximum that is adjusted annually. (Technically, 1.2 percent of that 7.65 percent is a Medicare deduction, but the two are lumped together. The income cap doesn't apply to the Medicare deduction.) Your employer is required to match

that, bringing the actual contribution up to 15.3 percent. As long as the social security fund remains on schedule to run out in 2030, it will remain a political hot potato. Regardless, the only thing you can do about it is hope that by the time you get to the front of the line there's still something left in the pot.

● *State income tax:* Traditionally the federal government has viewed the states as fifty spoiled children in need of discipline, while the states view Washington as an insecure parent that just can't let go. You, as a taxpayer, pay for that dysfunction with a state income tax levied on top of a federal tax. (Note: not all states charge an income tax.) Deductions and credits can lower your state income tax as well.

May Day!

For all your father's grumbling about tax-crazy politicians, he may have a point. Every year the Tax Foundation calculates how many days of the year the average taxpayer works just to pay his taxes. As of this writing, "Tax Freedom Day"—the point in the calendar where the money you earn is yours to keep—falls on May 3. Compare that to Freedom Days of years past:

Year	Tax Freedom Day
1930	February 13
1940	March 8
1950	April 3
1960	April 17
1970	April 28
1980	April 28
1990	May 3
2000	May 3

Kinda makes you want to call in sick till June, doesn't it?

Source: Tax Foundation.

- *State disability insurance:* Some states require your employer to carry insurance that covers you in the event you become incapacitated outside of the workplace. (Worker's Comp covers accidents that occur on the worksite.) The deduction on your pay stub (usually small) is your copayment. You can apply the total for the year to your medical deduction.
- *City income tax:* Many local governments have their own tax. Nothing you can do about these, but you can lump it in with your state and take it as a deduction (more on this later).

THE FIRST STEP TO MORE MONEY: CHOOSING THE RIGHT 1040

Your tax savings begins with the form you use. As the first step to getting your tax life in order, it can make a big difference in your final tax bill. There is no "one-size-fits-all" form for twenty-somethings: you must review the advantages each offers and then decide which best suits your own situation.

Fortunately, determining the best form is pretty simple. Once you know which one to use, you can get a copy by calling the IRS or stopping by your local post office. You can also download the forms directly from the IRS Web site (www.irs.gov).

Here's a rundown of your three tax form choices:

The 1040EZ: Think of the 1040EZ as a tax form with training wheels: use this form and the only other form you need is your W-2. No receipts, records, or schedules to attach. Not everyone is eligible to use this form, and even among those who can, not everyone should. To be EZ eligible, you must be single or married filing jointly (doesn't that sound like a TV show?) and your taxable income must be less than $50,000. You can't claim any dependents, and you cannot have taxable interest over $400. If you meet all of these criteria and don't have enough deductions to make itemizing worthwhile, this is the form for you. Grab a pen, take the standard deduction, and drop your return in the mail. Meet your other EZ friends April 14 and laugh at the rest of us stuck in tax paperwork hell.

The 1040A: Only slightly more difficult than the 1040EZ, the 1040A form has no maximum for taxable interest and allows you to claim limited deductions and credits. It also allows you to claim dependents. It has the same earned income restrictions as the 1040EZ. Unlike the EZ, here you can deduct your IRA contribution, student loan interest, and certain child-care and dependent-care expenses. You will have to attach additional schedules that show how you arrived at your figures. The 1040A still entitles you to a standard deduction regardless of how many other eligible deductions you take, but it is substantially lower than the 1040EZ standard deduction. Make sure the expenses you deduct on the 1040A are large enough to justify taking the smaller standard deduction.

The 1040: If your tax situation is too complicated to pass the restrictions of the 1040EZ or 1040A forms, congratulations— you've graduated to the tax big leagues. This is the form most people use, either because they have to, or because they can do better by itemizing than taking the standard deduction. For people with significant deductible expenses, this form is usually far more rewarding than the 1040EZ or 1040A. Yes, you'll have to roll up your sleeves and sort through the shoebox stuffed with last year's receipts, but a look at the box on the next page shows you one example of how that extra effort can pay off.

Are You Status Conscious?

Your tax rate is determined by more than just your income. The government sorts taxpayers into five different groups and applies different rates to each. In the majority of cases, a glance at your ring finger will help you narrow your options. If you are in an uncommon situation (for example, you fell in love junior year abroad and imported Jean-Paul to be your lawfully wedded husband), you should check out IRS Publication 17 to determine which status applies to your situation. The rest of you are easier to categorize.

LISTEN UP! No-brainer Savings Advice

Henry is twenty-two, one year out of college, and part of what he jokingly calls the "working poor." With no assets, heavy student loans, and a magazine job that pays $22,000, Henry assumes that he should use the same 1040EZ form that got him through his college years. However, if Henry took the time to tabulate his expenses, he would see that the 1040EZ is actually costing him money.

Henry's medical expenses, while significant, are hardly unique. His insurance plan only covers a small percentage of his therapy sessions, leaving Henry to cover $75 a week out of his own pocket. He wears contact lenses ($250), sees his dentist twice a year ($200), and can't get by without his Prozac ($780 after insurance reimbursement). Though his employer picks up most of the tab for Henry's health insurance, he contributes $545 through weekly deductions. He bought a new computer and printer last year, which he uses for work 90 percent of the time ($1,400), and donated three bags of old clothes to the Salvation Army ($300). Somehow, he also manages to squirrel away $2,000 to put into an IRA.

Now take a look at how Henry fares using the three different forms:

	1040EZ	1040A	1040
Total Income	$22,000	$22,000	$22,000
IRA	—	(2,000)	(2,000)
Adjusted Gross Income	22,000	20,000	20,000
Personal Exemption	2,750	2,750	2,750

Charitable Contributions	—	—	300
Medical Expenses	—	—	5,675
Miscellaneous Expenses	—	—	1,000
Total Itemized Deduction or Standard Deduction (whichever is greater)	4,300	4,300	6975
Exemption Plus Deductions	7,050	7,050	9,725
Taxable Income	14,950	12,950	10,275
TAX OWED (FEDERAL)	2,241	1,942	1,541

What a difference one little form can make!

Single. No kids, no spouse, no problem. Check single and read no further. (Actually, there is an exception: if you are taking care of a relative, you may qualify as Head of Household, which may save you money. If this applies to you, read on.)

Married Filing Jointly. Under joint filing, your income and your spouse's are treated as one income and taxed accordingly. You must also combine your deductions. As long as you were married at some point during the applicable tax year, you can still file jointly—even if you are currently separated or your spouse is deceased. Most married couples choose to file jointly, even though it may put them at risk for the dreaded "marriage penalty" (see box on page 120).

Married Filing Separately. This category has the highest tax rates, so it should be approached with caution. Generally, it should only be used if one spouse has substantially higher income and deductions. That's because certain expenses must surpass a percentage of your income before they become eligible to deduct. Since, in a joint return, the percentage is based on the combined total, the deductions would have to meet a higher ceiling before becoming eligible. For example, say a husband and wife both earn $50,000 a year, and the husband had an operation that cost $5,000. (For the purposes of this example assume it is their only medical expense.) If they filed separately, he would be entitled to take anything over $3,750 as a medical deduction. But if the couple filed jointly they would only be able to deduct expenses over $7,500, making the operation nondeductible. Be aware that should you decide to file separately, you and your spouse must be consistent in choosing to itemize or take the standard deduction. You are not allowed to select one of each.

Head of Household. If you are raising a child or caring for a family member alone, filing as Head of Household will generally lower your tax rate more than filing Single will. To qualify, the family member must have lived in your home for at least half the year *and* you must have paid at least half of the cost of maintaining your home. Head of Household can also apply to married individuals. If you and your spouse haven't lived together for at least half the year and children are involved, you may qualify. See IRS Publication 17 for further requirements.

For Richer or for Poorer: The "Marriage Penalty"

"Do you promise to love, honor, cherish, and pay more taxes 'til death do you part?" Much has been written about the strange glitch in the tax code that causes many married couples to pay more in taxes than their single selves. If you're planning a walk down the aisle in the near future, you should understand why you may come back from your honeymoon with a great tan and a smaller paycheck.

Although the penalty seems blatantly antifamily (after all, it takes money out of the pockets of new families who probably need it most), it was actually a post–World War II attempt to restore the traditional family by shaking women from the wartime workforce. Congress sought to reward families dependent on a single income and punish those with two working partners.

Though the one-income family is fast going the way of Diana Ross's singing career, Washington hasn't quite kept up with the times. (At the time of this writing, congressional Republicans were working on a bill that would address the marriage penalty. But, this being an election year, don't hold your breath expecting bipartisan cooperation.)

Here's how it works: say you're single and earn $40,000 a year. You fall head over heels for the woman who shares your workstation, and after a clandestine office romance you stun your coworkers with a wedding announcement. She has the exact same job as you do and makes the same salary, $40,000. As singles, you would be taxed at a 15 percent marginal tax rate on the first $25,350 of your salary and then 28 percent on the remaining $14,650. After you tie the knot, however, you usually file jointly, and your partner's income is considered an extension of yours. Her tax rate *begins* where yours leaves off (in this case, 28 percent), so the first dollar she earns is taxed at the higher rate. If that weren't enough to depress you on the big day, remember that higher incomes are also ineligible for many deductions and exemptions. If both you and your spouse work, you will reach those levels much more quickly.

Not every couple winds up paying higher taxes. If one of you doesn't work or makes substantially less than your spouse, you will actually pay less than if you were both single. That's small consolation to the twenty-one million couples who do pay more. Congress is coming under increasing pressure to change the law; however, when it comes to tax reform, the IRS is more tortoise than hare. Don't expect any drastic overhaul in the near future.

Qualifying Widow(er) with Dependent Child. If your spouse died this year and you have not remarried, you are entitled to file a joint return. If your spouse died earlier, you may still be able to file jointly if you have a dependent child. See IRS Publication 17 for details.

LOWERING YOUR TAXABLE INCOME

Under almost any circumstances, investing if you carry high-interest debt is a bad idea. Most investments, even the high-rolling stock market, rarely return more than you're paying to service high-interest debt. The system is stacked against you. It rewards the solvent and punishes the debt-ridden.

However, there is one exception to our rule. It's an investment that rewards you so well that regardless of your situation, we strongly recommend you jump on board. We're talking about the 401(k) plan, and here's how it works: Your company allows you to deduct a certain percentage of your income each week that is funneled into an investment strategy that you design. (Employees of public schools and charitable agencies may be eligible for a 403(b) plan.) You benefit in two important ways:

1. The money you put into the 401(k) plan lowers your total taxable income, which not only puts you in a lower tax bracket but may make you eligible for a host of deductions you might not qualify for otherwise.
2. The money you put into a 401(k) plan isn't taxed until you withdraw from the account. This is major. Every dollar you put in can grow untouched for years, as opposed to your lower, post-tax investments.

With a 401(k) plan, you only pay taxes on the back end, which means you've earned interest on all that pre-tax money over the years instead of the punier, IRS-deflated post-tax income. Over the years that can make a huge difference in the final payout. And when you consider that many employers match your contribution by as much as 50 percent, you will never come closer to a guaranteed winner than a 401(k) plan. Compare the difference in two identical investments, one in the safe haven of a 401(k), the other subject to taxes:

	401(k)	Taxable
TOTAL CONTRIBUTION	$100,000	$100,000
Less Taxes (33%)	0	33,333
Employer's matching contribution (contribution will vary)	50,000	0
Total available for investment	$150,000	66,666
Total return after 20 years (assume 10% annual return)	$429,563	$190,904

Of course, you will eventually be taxed on the $429,563, but you still come out miles ahead of the taxable account return.

If you work for a company that doesn't offer a 401(k) plan, don't despair. IRAs, or Investment Retirement Accounts, offer you the same opportunity to defer taxes on your contribution until you withdraw the funds. You get many of the same benefits as a 401(k) plan, with the following important differences:

- IRAs have a much lower maximimum allowable contribution than 401(k)s. You can contribute up to a maximum $2,000 a year into an IRA (and up to an additional $2,000 if your spouse doesn't work, with phase-outs based on income). However, with a 401(k) plan, you can contribute a percentage of your income up to a maximum of $10,500 a year. This distinction may not mean that much to you in your twenties (who has $10,000 sitting around to invest?), but it will as your income increases.
- Your employer does not contribute to your IRA contribution. With an IRA, the only money that grows is your own.
- In most cases, you are investing after-tax dollars with an IRA. As the table above shows, this is an extremely important difference. Once your money is in the IRA, however, the money grows tax-free just like it does in the 401(k).
- Unless you're single with an adjusted gross income (AGI)

under $25,000 or married filing jointly with an AGI under $40,000, you can't deduct your full IRA contribution from your taxable income. Depending on your circumstances, you may be entitled to a partial deduction.

It should be clear now that 401(k) plans are almost always the way to go. If your employer doesn't offer one, show him this book and suggest he begin one. Remind him that the costs of administering a 401(k) plan will be offset by the special tax breaks the government gives employers who participate (not to mention increased employee morale and loyalty).

A Note to the Self-employed

Great fortunes are made by those who strike out on their own. Bill Gates, Martha Stewart, Oprah Winfrey (she owns her show)— each took a gamble, did their own thing, and made out big time. If you don't work for yourself, no matter how well you're compensated, you are hired to make money for somebody else, be it the boss or shareholders. Most of us at some point dream about the day we can take control of our own destiny. With that entrepreneurial freedom, however, comes a different set of rules that you must abide by if you want to stay on the IRS's good side.

The biggest bummer to being your own boss is that, as both employer and employee, you are responsible for the entire FICA contribution. That's 15 percent right off the bat, which can be a real burden in the early days of building a business. As a self-employed person, you also lose the tax breaks of a 401(k) plan, since they are usually only available to employees of larger corporations.

You can partially remedy this by opening a traditional IRA, or if you want to be a really aggressive saver, consider a SEP-IRA or a Keogh. Both are retirement plans for the self-employed that offer the same tax advantages as a traditional IRA but with substantially higher saving caps.

A SEP-IRA, or simplified employee pension, allows you to

contribute a percentage of your first $170,000 of net earnings. That's a maximum of $22,500 compared to the $2,000 limit of a traditional IRA. Keoghs (pronounced "Key-Oh") are considerably more complicated, but they allow you to save even more money than a SEP. One caveat: for both plans, if you have employees you may have to earmark part of your contribution for them as well.

Finally, if being your own boss didn't carry enough responsibility already, the IRS expects you to take taxes into your own hands. Since there is no boss to do the withholding for you, the IRS requires you to estimate your taxes every three months and send them a check. It is important to estimate as accurately as possible. If you underestimate too wildly, you may be hit with penalties and interest.

Penalize This

You learned a long time ago that procrastinating not only makes things worse, it makes things more expensive. Taxes are not unlike bills that accumulate on your shelf or that odd rash you noticed in the shower—they don't just disappear if you ignore them. In the case of paying taxes, April 15 is the line in the sand. Those who get the magic postmark can kick back and congratulate themselves for not making taxes any more expensive than necessary. Those who miss the deadline face a whirl of harsh penalties and interest rates that may mire you in the tax tarpit for many months to come.

The easiest way to protect yourself from this ugliness is to file your return and pay all taxes you owe by April 15. The IRS is notoriously unsympathetic to latepayers and if you even try to make an excuse for your tardiness you'll be met with the government equivalent of "talk to the hand." Fail to file and the IRS will tack on a penalty of 5 percent of the amount you owe every month until you pay, up to a maximum of 25 percent. You will also be assessed a variable interest rate (usually between 7 and 10 percent) until you pay. (There is no cap on the amount of interest you are liable for.)

If you simply need more time to get your return ready, you can request a filing extension. You should apply before April 15. The extension allows you to file your return up until August 15, but you still must estimate your tax bill and send payment by April 15 to avoid interest charges. Make sure your estimate is close to the actual tax bill. If you underestimate by more than 10 percent, you'll be hit with additional penalties and interest.

If you simply don't have the money to pay, you can reduce the penalties and fees by paying on the installment plan. You still must send in your return by April 15, but instead of sending a check with it, include IRS Form 9465, which is a formal application for the installment plan. In all likelihood you will be approved, but not without some pain. Besides a one-time processing fee of $43, you will still have to pay penalties and interest, although they will be far smaller than if you don't file at all. To avoid the same trauma next year, consider taking fewer exemptions if you expect your income to be roughly the same as this year's.

How to Avoid a Tax Audit

In recent years, much has been written about the transformation of the IRS from an angry grizzly into something considerably more soft and fuzzy. Televised congressional testimony from abused taxpayers left the IRS with a serious image problem it is now taking great pains to rehabilitate. Much of the bullying and enforcement tactics of the past have been replaced by a more hospitable organization. Still, regardless of how honest and scrupulous you are in filing, your tax return is like a work of art—open to interpretation and subject to criticism.

Though in recent years the IRS has cut back on the percentage of taxpayers targeted for auditing, that won't matter much to you if you open a letter that begins "Dear Taxpayer." Despite what you may have heard, audits are not all selected randomly. Many different factors influence your odds of being audited. Some, such as where you live, you have little control over. (Did you know someone living in Los Angeles is many times more likely to be audited than someone from Brooklyn? Must be revenge for stealing the Dodgers.)

However, there is a lot you can do to make an audit someone else's problem. The IRS has a limited staff to chase down taxpayers it suspects of underreporting. Therefore, they rely on past experience of taxpayer behavior and statistics to catch likely underreporters. Knowing the biggest auditing red flags won't guarantee you'll escape an IRS audit, but it will greatly improve your chances of disappearing into the crowd.

The home office deduction: At first glance, this sounds like a great deduction. It allows you to deduct a percentage of your rent or mortgage based on the square footage of your home office. On the downside, you greatly enhance the risk of a field agent showing up at your house unannounced with a yardstick and a camera. Not a fun way to kick off a Saturday. Worse, if your return is pulled for one suspicious deduction, the entire return is subject to scrutiny. That's a big gamble many people just don't want to take.

You could argue that since you legitimately use a part of your home as an office, you are perfectly entitled to take the deduction. And you're right. Unfortunately, you may spend considerable time and money proving to the IRS how right you are, while answering any other questions your audit raises. You may very well win the battle and lose the war.

We recommend taking the home office deduction only if you can establish beyond a reasonable doubt that a part of your house is used strictly for business. A record-keeping system verging on the anal can't hurt either. If you qualify on both counts, try to stave off an audit by attaching a letter to your return (preferably on office stationery that bears your home address) explaining the deduction.

Excessive charitable deductions: If you remember those less fortunate than yourself, you're a good person. But if you donate your crappy old bicycle to your church and call it a Land Rover on your return, the IRS will hunt you down. After the home deduction, probably nothing raises the IRS's eyebrows more quickly than disproportionate giving in relation to income.

The IRS keeps a table of average charitable contributions for each income tax bracket. The percentage varies based on income level. This doesn't mean you should let the IRS determine how generous you are with your money, but if you are more giving than the average Joe, a few precautions are in order. Get a receipt from every institution you contribute to, and just as important, attach the originals to your return. This will show the certifier the deductions are legitimate before it gets to the audit stage. (Don't forget to keep a copy for yourself.)

Unreimbursed employee business expenses: When it comes to unreimbursed employee deductions, the IRS's philosophy is "if the boss wouldn't allow it, why should we?" You may think that weekend rock climbing with your office buddies is a valid business expense since you talked trash about the boss, but the IRS sees things a little differently. The IRS knows that workers tend to be lazy when it comes to documenting these expenses, so challenging them usually results in easy money for the government. For a twentysomething with few other places to deduct, this area can prove extremely tempting to fudge. Proceed with caution. For a list of allowable employee deductions, see IRS form 535.

Cash may be king, but it's anathema to the IRS: It's not hard to see why—with no paper trail to keep you honest, it becomes tough to "remember" to report every dollar. If you fall into a profession with untraceable income potential, they will do their best at making sure you remember. Independent contractors, doctors, performers, small business owners, and writers (hey!) are a few of the occupations the IRS views with suspicion. Fairly or unfairly, these professions get a little extra unwanted attention from the IRS.

Prepare wisely: Earlier we recommended doing your own taxes once you get the hang of it. There is one exception to this rule, and it's an important one to keep in mind if you don't want to set off the audit trigger. If you have an elaborate return involving fancy terms like "credit shelter trusts" and "limited liability partnerships," use a reputable tax preparer. If you attempt to save some money by doing your own taxes, not only will you probably get something wrong, the IRS will likely assume you did and pull your return for an audit. Better to spend the money on a professional and be a tightwad somewhere else.

Also, avoid any preparer who promises you the moon. The IRS targets preparers with a history of runaway creativity. If you use one, you automatically increase your chance of an audit. The IRS doesn't disclose their list of overzealous preparers, so use your instincts. Ask other people who have used him or her. If you hear, "Every year he gets thousands of dollars more than I expected" too many times, run, don't walk, to someone a little more restrained.

Treat your mortgage application as a tax return: That little white lie on your loan application could come back to haunt you. As IRS computers increase the agency's compliance efficiency, they have become much more agile at cross-referencing your tax return with other personal information floating in cyberspace. If the computer catches an inconsistency between the income you claim on a loan application and your return, they know you are lying on at least one of the documents and will move in for the kill. Even if the income listed on your return is the right one, the IRS assumes that you are an innately duplicitous person and will root through your return for other lies. Take this one seriously—cross-referencing has proved very successful in nailing underreporters.

None of these suggestions is meant to obscure the best defense against an audit—honesty and scrupulous documentation. That being said, an unfavorably adjusted return, even one resulting from honest mistakes or incomplete records, can be financially disastrous. Most people leave an audit owing money, money that often includes hefty interest and penalties. It's simply smart policy to take a few sensible precautions before you file than risk a tax nightmare down the road. Trust me on this, audits are no fun. In my early twenties, when I was struggling on $25,000 a year in New York City, I received a letter from the IRS informing me that the hotel restaurant where I had worked in college had been audited and I owed $2,300 in back taxes. The IRS found that the owner (amusingly enough, a guy who had been convicted in the Studio 54 tax evasion scandal) hadn't withheld the proper amount of tax for the entire staff, and we were all responsible for making up the difference.

Although it turned out to be an innocent hotel accounting error, the IRS hit the employees with substantial interest and penalties. The experience was devastating—I was already in debt and had no idea how I would come up with that kind of money on my salary. Worse, I was assigned to an inexperienced agent who couldn't answer my most basic questions. My only choice was to pay up or hire an attorney. The experience taught me how expensive ignorance could be.

The Big Deductions . . .

Finally, the fun stuff. Fasten your seatbelts, because here's where the ride gets veerrrryyy interesting. Here are some of the most common deductions that can help you take a big bite out of your tax bill.

State and local income taxes: If you live somewhere with a state income tax, here's your chance to partially even the score against those who don't. You can deduct the entire amount of your state and local (either county or city or both) income tax bill from your federal return. For most of us, this will lower our taxable income by thousands of dollars in one fell swoop, so this is one not to miss. Enter this deduction on line 5 of schedule A.

Some local taxes other than income are deductible, but many are not. No doubt you've heard some relative yammering on about how you're flushing your money down the toilet if you rent. This is because of the endless tax breaks homeowners get.

Homeowners get to deduct all property taxes on their home (whether it's a house or co-op). If you do own a home and you haven't been hit with a property tax bill, don't assume you got lucky and slipped through the cracks. All that means is your mortgage holder has lumped your taxes in with your mortgage payments and paid the government directly. Your mortgage statement will tell you the exact amount allotted for taxes. Enter that amount on line 6 of schedule A.

Taxes on personal property can often be deductible, but figuring out which ones are can take some work. The rule of thumb is if the tax is based on the item's *value* it may be deductible. If it is not, it is considered a fee and therefore not eligible. Huh? For example, if you live in a state that assesses a personal property tax on your car, you can deduct the tax. However, if you drive a Civic and paid the same bill as your neighbor with the new Mercedes, the charge is a flat tax and not based on the car's value. Therefore it is non-deductible. Also, don't assume that the entire bill can be written off even if it is linked to value. The total may contain such non-deductible items as license renewal fee. Only the tax portion of the bill is eligible.

Mortgage: Another reason homeowners win the tax race: as an owner, you can deduct all of the interest on your mortgage, regardless of the rate. (The principal portion of your payment is non-deductible.) The IRS doesn't care who you paid the interest to, so if your parents offered you a better deal than First National, you can still deduct the interest. New homeowners still recovering from "points" shock (the one-time fee for borrowing money from a lender) will be partially relieved to know that they can lump that in with mortgage interest. Enter the total amount on line 10 of schedule A.

Medical expenses: Finally, a deduction for hypochondriacs. If your only health-related bills last year consisted of two trips to the doctor and a bottle of Tylenol, you can stop right here. The IRS allows you to deduct certain medical expenses, but only those that exceed 7.5 percent of your AGI. For example, if your AGI last year was $30,000, you could deduct any qualifying medical expense over $2,250 (30,000 × .075). Any amount reimbursed by insurance doesn't count.

While the list of eligible medical expenses is far too long to include here, the general rule is if you can get a prescription for it, you can write it off. For doctor visits, if you see a diploma on the wall from a medical school, you can probably deduct the visit. Don't automatically assume your medical bills won't exceed the limit. Contact lenses, health insurance, birth control—those bills add up more quickly than you think, and they're all deductible. If you see a therapist, for example, chances are your health plan doesn't pick up the entire tab. Depending on your income, those weekly sessions alone may put your expenses over the 7.5 percent deduction.

Capital losses: So that tip you got from your cousin, the Wall Street hotshot, didn't exactly catch fire. You can either give him the cold shoulder at Thanksgiving or you can deduct your loss from your taxes. That goes for most other investments besides stocks, too.

LISTEN UP! No-brainer Savings Advice

Although you can't carry over medical expenses from year to year, try to lump the big bills together in one calendar year to reach the 7.5 percent deduction level. For example, if you're planning to have your eyes lasered in January and you had expensive dental work in May, doing the eye surgery in December instead may save you money on your taxes.

...And a Dozen Smaller Ones You May Not Know About

Late charges on mortgage payments: Need any further proof that the government hates renters? Homeowners late with the mortgage payment get to lump any penalties in with their tax-deductible interest. Renters late with the rent get evicted.

On-line brokerage interest: When you buy a stock on margin, you are borrowing money to invest. Your on-line broker charges interest for the privilege, but you get to deduct the interest regardless of whether the stock goes up or down.

Take a meeting at the beach: If you're willing to mix some business with pleasure, you'll come home with more money in your pocket for next year's vacation. While the last thing anyone wants to do is think about the office when they're 3,000 miles away from it, the tax savings can prove too good to pass up. If you can prove the trip is primarily for business and your employer is not reimbursing you, you can deduct all transportation and lodging costs, as well as half of the meal and entertainment expenses on the days you work.

If you want to take a long weekend somewhere, one meeting Friday and another one Monday gives you a tax deductible Saturday and Sunday. Now what's more relaxing than that? (Don't forget to keep any documentation that supports your case. Receipts, diaries, and correspondence are generally considered sufficient proof that one can tan and work simultaneously.)

Party with your boss: It's one of the hardest lessons of post-college life: Doritos and Corona for eighty of your nearest and dearest ain't cheap. But mix in a couple of co-workers and associates, call it a business affair, and you can knock the whole thing off your taxes.

The IRS doesn't specify an exact friend to business ratio, but you must be prepared to prove that it was primarily a business function. Keep a copy of the guest list, as well as photocopies of the addressed envelopes that you used to mail the invitations. Posting a guest sign-in book by the door is a great way to prove your case (and your guests will never know what you're up to).

Make student loans less interest-ing: The U.S. government, never known for extending much sympathy for downtrodden college students (remember how bitter you were that you had to pay income tax on your pathetic work-study wages), is finally giving graduates a break with a recent change in tax policy. If you make less than $40,000 a year ($60,000 for married couples), you can deduct up to $1,500 in student loan interest. You don't even have to itemize to qualify.

A Lifetime of Hope: Though technically not a deduction, these tax breaks are so good we had to mention them somewhere. The Hope Scholarship is a tax credit that allows college students to lop $1,500 off their taxes for the first two years of college. This credit is actually better than a deduction: where a deduction lowers the income that is subject to taxes, a credit is more like an immediate cash-back coupon. A student who worked part-time and owed $2,000 in federal taxes would, after the Hope Scholarship, owe only $500.

If you've already got a diploma collecting dust in your attic, you can still save money and broaden your mind. The Lifetime Learning Credit grants a $1,000 credit ($2,000 beginning in 2002) for post-college education, regardless of subject matter. The catch: once again, if you're single, you have to make $40,000 or less ($80,000 for married couples). If you make more, you may still be eligible for a smaller exemption.

Stop smoking, get richer: For years, the IRS didn't allow smokers to deduct the costs of trying to break the nicotine habit. Now, the IRS has decided that it wants you to live longer (maybe so you can pay more taxes). Reformed smokers can now apply many of their expenses toward the medical expense allowance. (Your medical expenses still must reach 7.5 percent of your AGI to qualify.) What's covered: prescription drugs, hospital cessation programs, and doctor bills. What's not: nonprescription treatments, which includes nicotine patches and chewing gums such as Nicorette.

Tax preparation expenses: In the eyes of the IRS, anything that helps with your taxes is considered worthy of a deduction. This includes tax preparation software, books like this one (hope you saved the receipt!), tax preparer fees, even the cost of copying your returns at the local Kinko's. The same holds true for investment materials, so write off that Motley Fool book you bought last year! And no, they don't care that you never read it.

Cell phones, computers, ISPs, and phone lines: Technojunkies rejoice! The rules governing what you can deduct are pretty straightforward: whatever percentage of the expense you use for your job is considered a business expense and therefore deductible. For example, a phone call to check in with your office is tax deductible; a call to your girlfriend to tell her how much you love her is not. If you use a flat-rate calling plan, you get to deduct whatever percentage you use for business.

Computers and ISPs fall under the same guidelines: feel free to deduct whatever percentage you use for professional purposes, but be smart about it. Keep a log of the time spent surfing the Web for work. If you deduct 100 percent of the cost of a new computer, you are claiming that you never once played a game of Tetris, answered a personal E-mail, or ordered anything from petopia.com. The IRS may have a hard time swallowing that one.

Telephone deductions are a bit more complicated. Only long-distance calls that are work-related can be deducted from your primary line. Local calls and the monthly service charge cannot. However, if you have a second line that you use strictly for business, you can deduct the entire cost, including all service charges, fees, and taxes.

Moving: On the stress meter, moving ranks a close third to death and divorce. The IRS eases the pain by allowing you to deduct certain expenses if you are relocating for a new job. However, only certain moves are covered. To be eligible, your *new job* must be at least fifty miles farther from your *old house* than your *old job* was. Got that?

In other words, if the difference between House A and Job A is ten miles, Job B must be at least sixty miles away from House A to qualify for the moving deduction. (It might be easier to do what you did on the SATs for those impossible math questions—draw a picture in the margins.) You must also stay at the new job for at least thirty-nine weeks of the first year after the move.

What's fair game? You can deduct the bill for the moving company, all packing supplies, and the tip to the moving guys who lugged your sofa up three flights of stairs. You can also deduct any traveling and lodging expenses incurred during the actual move. Of course, if your employer pays for the move, you can't take the deduction.

Casualty and theft losses: This is one deduction we hope you never have to take, but if misfortune should strike, this deduction might help you get back on your feet. Unfortunately, your personal loss must be substantial before you qualify for any kind of tax break. The IRS permits you to deduct any loss above 10 percent of your adjusted gross income, less $100 for each incident. This law is intended to protect against catastrophes only. If your only loss last year was the chair your dog chewed, you don't qualify. If insurance partially covers your loss, only the unreimbursed difference is eligible for the deduction.

If you take this deduction, collect everything pertaining to the incident—police reports, receipts, photographs, newspaper articles, etc.—so you will be fully prepared if the IRS asks for further documentation.

Charity: Time is money, but not when it comes to charity or volunteer work. You cannot assign a "fair wage" to the hours you commit to a good cause and deduct it from your return. However, you can deduct certain expenses you incur while volunteering. Mileage, postage, parking, and tolls all qualify. Save all receipts, and if you use your car as either transportation to the charity or for a function (say, to deliver meals to the disadvantaged), keep a log of when and where you drove.

Don't Even Try It

Not only are the following expenses nondeductible, you could find yourself in hot water should the IRS figure out what you're up to.

Double-dipping: If your employer reimburses you for certain business expenses, don't claim them on your return. Since your employer will take the deduction, it is extremely easy for the IRS to catch you.

Vet bills: Your pet may be like a child to you, but he's still got four legs and a tail. Vet bills and animal prescriptions cannot be tallied to meet the medical expense deductible. (In case you were wondering, they can't be claimed as dependents either.)

A fake business: Yes, tax laws favor the self-employed. As your own boss, more of your life becomes deductible. With this in mind, some people are tempted to claim they run a business just for the tax savings. If you helped a friend move one Saturday and he paid you in pizza, you cannot claim to run a moving company on the side. The IRS has strict rules governing that sort of thing. With the time you spend (rightly) worrying about getting caught, why not start a real business instead?

Interest on credit cards: If only. As recently as the eighties you could charge that fetching Member's Only jacket and matching parachute pants on your parent's Visa and they wouldn't mind because they could deduct the interest from their taxes. Sadly, those days have gone the way of Jennifer Beals. The IRS no longer subsidizes your bad habits.

Clothing: Unless you wear a uniform, you usually cannot deduct the clothes you wear to work. The IRS is unbending on this one. Even if your employer requires you to wear black pants and a white shirt, if they are clothes you would conceivably wear on your downtime, you can't deduct them.

THE IRS PIGGY BANK

Many money managers will advise that you have the IRS withhold no more money than necessary from your paycheck every week. After all, if you're just going to get the money back after April 15, it's like giving the government an interest-free loan. You could be using the money to pay down your debt instead. And intellectually, that makes sense. Unfortunately, when it comes to matters of the wallet, we know the brain is probably one of the lesser-utilized organs.

Having the IRS withhold a few extra dollars a week is a great way to plow money into your personal debt reduction plan. Yes, you'll be out the interest, but you'll also be spared fifty-two weeks of temptation to piss away that money at the mall. Consider lowering the number of exemptions on your W-2 form or allotting a dollar amount next to the line marked "Additional amount you want withheld."

REFUNDS ARE FOREVER

Not quite, but not many people know that the IRS makes it simple to apply for a retroactive refund if you've overpaid in the past. As long as you file no later than three years from the due date of the year in question *or* two years from the time you paid the tax (whichever is later), you could be eligible for not only money owed to you but the interest as well. This is a potential windfall for the formerly tax clueless. Inexperience with taxes can easily cause many young people to skip a deduction or make some other mistake.

Many people just starting out assume that they don't make enough money to itemize, so they file form 1040EZ on April 14 and forget about taxes until next year. However, as you now know, just because it's EZ doesn't make it right. Depending on your individual situation, even someone making $21,000 a year might benefit from itemizing. After I learned that I could file for a retroactive return, I combed through my EZ years and discovered that itemizing would have netted me more money. I filed an amended return and got almost $1,000 back. Not enough to make me rich, but a nice dent in my credit cards. Another friend did the same and got $3,200 back. So get a little nostalgic and break out your returns for the past three years. If you follow what you learned in this chapter, you might be in for an early Christmas present from the government.

How to File an Amended Return

Squeezing money out of past returns is actually a fairly simple process. To get a quick response from the IRS, follow these simple steps:

1. *Request form 1040X from the IRS.* You can do this by calling or downloading it from the IRS's website. You must fill out a separate form for each year you are requesting a refund.
2. *Attach all documents that relate to the specific amendment.* For example, if you are claiming a higher amount for a deduction that requires a specific IRS form, include a new form with the changes.
3. *Include a letter explaining why you are entitled to a refund.* You should also tell the IRS the amount you feel you are entitled to, along with the phrase "Or such greater amount as is legally refundable, with interest." This obligates the IRS to pay up in case they calculate a bigger refund than you've requested.

One caveat: When you file an amended return, you run the risk that the IRS might spot something they didn't catch the first time. You should be confident your return can withstand a second review *before* you file an amended return.

ADDITIONAL HELP

We've tried to be as up-to-the-minute and accurate as possible in this chapter. However, tax codes are hopelessly complex and constantly evolving. It would take a tome much larger than this chapter to thoroughly explain the fine print regarding every deduction, exemption, or restriction. If you choose to go it alone this tax season, request any of the following free publications from the IRS that may apply to you (call 1-800-TAX-FORM or download them from the IRS Web site). Most of the publications are under twenty pages and fairly easy to understand. Following them will ensure that you get back the proper amount owed to you.

Publication No.		
	4	Student's Guide to Federal Taxes
	17	Your Federal Income Tax
	501	Exemptions, Standard Deductions, and Filing Information
	502	Medical and Dental Expenses
	505	Tax Withholding and Estimated Tax
	508	Educational Expenses
	520	Scholarships and Fellowships
	521	Moving Expenses
	525	Taxable and Non-Taxable Income
	531	Reporting Tax Income
	552	Record Keeping for Individuals
	590	Individual Retirement Arrangements
	917	Business Use of a Car
	919	Is My Witholding Correct?

CHEAT SHEET

We all pay taxes. Smart people pay what they have to and not one penny more. By familiarizing yourself with basic tax rules, you can substantially lower your tax bill and free up that money to reduce your debt.

- *Seek professional help.* If you're intimidated by taxes, consider paying for the services of a tax preparer until you're more confident. The extra money she finds in your return will probably more than offset her fee.
- *Choose the right form.* Don't assume that just because you don't make much money, you should automatically use the 1040EZ form. Your deductions and exemptions may still be higher than the standard deduction.
- *Open a 401(k) account.* If your employer offers one, a 401(k) plan is one of the best ways to lower your taxable income *and* invest in the future. Even if you can't contribute much, the earlier you get started, the more time your money will have to grow.
- *Don't get greedy.* Be aware of the IRS audit triggers. Home office deductions, using an overaggressive accountant, and claiming excessive charitable deductions may raise the auditor's eyebrows.

8

Car(nal) Knowledge

WELCOME TO THE UNITED STATES OF AUTOMOBILES—LOVE IT OR LEAVE IT

We Americans love our cars. Once upon a time car drivers viewed their car as nothing more than a speedy way to get from point A to point B. In the 1920s Henry Ford could offer his model-T "in any color as long as it's black" and still sell a zillion of them. If he said that today, he would probably find himself working at the corner Amoco station instead.

For better or for worse, most Americans believe you are what you drive. Not only do our cars define who we are, but who we would like to be. We draw quick conclusions about people based on what sits in the driveway. Who would be more fun on a sun-drenched tropical getaway, the driver of a Volvo station wagon or a Porsche Boxster? Conversely, if you're looking for 2.2 kids and the white picket fence, who would you choose to settle down with for the long haul?

Does all of this car-centricity make you a superficial person? No. After all, you grew up immersed in car culture. What was the mother of all prizes on *The Price Is Right*, the dinette set or the Chevy Malibu? In *Risky Business*, Tom Cruise didn't sink his fa-ther's moped. And before you found your older brother's stash of

Playboys, you had to make do with the Vargas girl splayed across a silky red Corvette on the cover of a Cars album. You probably even thought "Little Red Corvette" was about a car.

So it's perfectly understandable that you crave far more car than you can afford. Unfortunately, after credit card abuse, big car dreams are probably the biggest cause of a twentysomething's financial downfall. Many newspaper and magazine articles laughably refer to a car as "the second biggest investment," after a house, you are likely to make. As an investment, you might have better luck investing in Russian rubles. What other investment practically guarantees it will lose at least 20 percent of its value after the first year, and a full 35–40 percent by year three? Worse, with average new car prices climbing well past the $20,000 mark, cars are gobbling up a higher percentage of incomes than ever before.

These days, there are as many choices to buying, financing, and maintaining a car as there are models. SUV or sports car? Lease or buy? Which options will make the car easier to sell? But if you have your heart set on a two ton steel-and-glass monster with a sticker price that can easily surpass a year's take-home salary, we have one piece of advice: Proceed very, very slowly. One wrong step can set you back hundreds or thousands of dollars.

In this chapter we answer the tough questions. Does the expense and trouble of driving a new car ultimately improve your quality of life? At what point do the liabilities of driving a new car outweigh the benefits? We also walk you through the entire car process, from buying or leasing your car, to maintaining it, to ultimately getting the most for it when it's time to say good-bye.

BUYING NEW: JUST SAY NO, NO, NO!

When you list the costs of driving a new car for one year, certain expenses immediately spring to mind. First, of course, there's the hefty downpayment, usually 20 percent of the purchase price. Since most of us can't write a check for 25 grand, we can expect to make monthly payments for the next three to five years. Insurance, too, with its institutional bias against young drivers, will put another big dent in your wallet. Then of course there's the regular recurring expenses like gas, oil changes, car washes, and so on, which can really add up. When you sit down and do the math, you might just discover why you're so broke at the end of each month.

The Depreciation Dilemma

If the number staring back at you doesn't make the bus start to look good, hold on, because you still haven't included the biggest cost of driving a new car. Expenses like fuel, insurance, and finance costs are easy to calculate because they are constantly in your face. But the biggest expense, depreciation, you don't even notice until you're ready to sell the car. By then it's too late—car dealerships don't give refunds.

A car's depreciation is defined as the difference between the price you paid for it minus the amount you recoup upon selling it. Four years after buying a new car, you're driving a vehicle that's shed on average half its value. And that's an average; many models fare even worse. For example, according to one study, a four-year-old Geo Metro two-door that cost $10,000 new will net you only $2,500—less than a business-class ticket between New York and L.A. Imagine if the house you scrimped and saved for lost 75 percent of its value after four years. You'd probably strangle your real estate broker. Yet when it comes to cars, most of us seem to accept the lousy economics as the price of suburban living.

Few big-ticket goods depreciate as fast as an automobile, yet each year Detroit still sells an awful lot of them. Status explains part of the demand, but ignorance about the perceived advantages of new versus used cars causes many people to make some expensive and misinformed decisions. Below are the most frequently cited justifications for forking over all that extra dough for a new car:

"I don't want to deal with the inconvenience of maintenance and repairs." In your parents' days of tail fins and whitewalls, there was some merit to this argument. Back then, keeping a car

running required a finely tuned schedule of fluids to check, plugs to change, and mufflers to replace. Fail to do any one of these and your parents most likely found themselves stranded roadside on prom night.

Well, times have changed, and in the words of one advertising jingle, "This is not your father's Oldsmobile." Responding to the stiff Japanese competition of the early eighties, cars simply got . . . better. When Honda, Toyota, and Datsun (now Nissan) raised the bar for fuel economy, style, and affordability, Detroit was forced to follow suit or perish. Today's cars live longer and need fewer tune-ups (the original 10,000 mile tune-up has been stretched to 50,000 and, in some cases, 100,000). One industry veteran estimates that people spend roughly 25 percent less on maintenance over the life of a car than in decades past.

Your own experience will vary with the model you drive and how well you treat it, but one thing is certain: no matter how much time your car spends at the repair shop, in the long run depreciation will always cost you more.

"*I like the peace of mind that comes with a new-car warranty.*" This is understandable up to a point. No one enjoys surprises—least of all ones that involve forking over $400 to the mechanic at the service station. A new car warranty protects you from unforeseen expenses. You don't have to worry about choosing between Christmas in South Beach or fixing your transmission.

The problem with this line of reasoning is that most of the hefty repairs—the kind you really want your warranty to stick around for—occur in the later years of a car's life. Like we said, cars really do run better now than ever before, so that three-year/36,000-mile warranty is much less valuable than it was even fifteen years ago. Of course, every car will have to spend some time in the repair shop, but nowadays it's far less than you think. What would be worth far more to you as a new car owner is a "delayed" warranty that kicked in *after* you've had the car a few years. But we all know automakers aren't that generous.

"Hey, it's a superficial world. I need a nice car so my boss and clients will take me seriously." Your boss and coworkers are more likely to be impressed with what you do while you're at the office than how you get there. Look at your calendar and come out of the eighties. The Mercedes-driving, Armani-suit-wearing Master of the Universe has been conquered by the 26-year-old Internet zillionaire who runs his kingdom in Nikes and shorts. Of course, appearances still count, but the workplace trend over the past couple years has been toward the decidedly more relaxed. Casual Fridays now often start on Wednesday, and the suit is becoming an endangered species in all but the most corporate settings.

The same attitude spills over to the parking lot. You simply don't need to spend more on your car than your parents spent on their first house to prove you're a player. This is not to say that you should pull up to an important lunch in a rusting '85 Yugo. But any clean, well-maintained used car is just fine for the new, dressed-down corporate America. If your boss has any common sense, he'll take note that you don't need your car to speak for you. No one ever got promoted because her car came from Bavaria. (The only exception to this is Hollywood, where what you drive is in fact much more important than whether or not you can even spell Bavaria.)

"A new car will help me meet girls." Wrong again. They'll just think you're compensating for something else.

LISTEN UP! No-brainer Savings Advice

If you've recently bought a new car, it's not too late to show the world your mama didn't raise no fool. Take good care of the car and you'll be able to drive it for years. The longer you hold on to it, the lower your annualized costs will be.

How to Buy a New Car
(Even Though We Told You Not To)

We hope we've made a strong case for buying used. But you've read all of the above and, depreciation be damned, you still want that new car. While we still say that cutting driving expenses is one of the easiest and effective ways to save money and get out of debt, we also promised you "no lectures." But beware. The new-car-buying journey is fraught with danger. By following the steps below, however, you can rest assured that the laughter you hear as you pull out of the car lot isn't coming from the salesperson.

Financing

One of the biggest mistakes you can make as a new-car buyer is to think your job is done once you've agreed on a price. You've done your homework, shopped around, and negotiated a tough deal with the salesperson, only to blow it when it comes time to pay for the damn thing. Since you will most likely be carrying the loan for as long as you own the car, you should give your loan the same thoughtful deliberation that went into your search. As you can see from the financing chart below, one little percentage point can make a big difference in the price of a car over the life of the loan. Below, we tell you what to do to get the best possible loan.

Shop around and get preapproved for a loan: This is the foundation upon which all good deals are built. All loans are not created equal. The last thing you want to do is accept a dealer's financing because it "sounds" fair. Depending on your credit history and other factors, sometimes banks or credit unions will offer you the lowest interest rate; other times the dealer will. Don't let the dealer persuade you that he offers the best terms in town. That may in fact be true, but ultimately it is your responsibility to verify.

Your credit union is a good place to start, since they often offer favorable rates to members. Call at least three banks (each call should take about five minutes) and compare rates. To get a solid idea of the range of interest rates, you should try one national bank, one regional bank, and your own, since some banks offer their account holders a "good customer" rate if you meet a minimum balance.

Once you've found the best rate, try to get preapproved for a loan. This is a simple process where a lender determines how much "borrowed car" you can handle and promises to lend you the money should you buy a car. It is usually a free service, and most banks will give you an answer the same day. You are under no obligation to accept the loan from that bank.

Getting preapproved for a loan offers several advantages. It lets the dealer know you are a serious shopper and that you can pay for the car. Remember, any schmo can walk into a showroom and announce that he wants to buy a new car. The salesperson will spend hours with him, explaining the car's features, haggling over the price, etc., only to run a credit check and discover that his customer can barely afford Rollerblades, let alone a car. Preapproval guarantees you will get more attention and possibly even a better price; the last thing any salesperson wants to do is let a qualified buyer slip out the door. Most important, it gives you the crucial "opening bid" where *you* set the number to beat instead of the reverse.

Steer clear of low downpayments and long repayment plans: We cannot stress this enough. Like those credit card balances that stay with you forever, the more you borrow and the longer you carry the loan, the more that car will ultimately cost you. Remember that the price you negotiate with the dealer isn't the final price of the car. Like the $6,265 iMac on page 76 in chapter five, you must calculate the years of interest-soaked monthly payments to determine the overall price of the car.

As new car prices continue to escalate, more and more people stretch the length of their car loan out over four, five, even six years. This keeps the monthly payments low, putting ordinarily unaffordable cars in reach. Don't fall into this trap. An extended loan will tie up your money longer, keeping another chunk of your paycheck committed to yet another creditor. You will also find yourself driving "upside down" longer than you would like, which is the term used to describe what happens when you owe more money than the car is worth. (Perhaps a better term might be DWI—Driving While Indebted.) The table below shows the total cost of a $20,000 new car under different financing terms.

	7%	8%	9%	10%	11%
3 years	$22,231	$22,562	$22,896	$23,232	$23,572
4 years	22,988	23,436	23,890	24,348	24,812
5 years	23,761	24,311	24,910	25,497	26,091
7 years	25,356	26,185	27,030	27,890	28,765

Since you can't sell the car without scraping up extra cash to pay off the loan, upside-down drivers sometimes find themselves chained to their cars for years. And as a repentant debtor your goal is financial freedom, so you want to keep your upside-down driving to an absolute minimum. The surest way to do this is to force yourself not to buy a new car until you've saved at least 20 percent for the downpayment and apply for a three-year loan, max. If the monthly payment is still out of your range, it's time to downsize your auto dreams.

A warning to the credit-scarred: If your credit report is less than squeaky-clean, chances are you're already used to paying higher rates to borrow money. However, that doesn't mean you should be resigned to the double-digit whopper the F&I (Finance & Insurance) department may try to stick you with. It's not uncommon for car dealers to prey on your vulnerability and insecurity about your credit history. They know that as a group the credit-damaged are often grateful for any loan they qualify for and often won't complain about outrageous interest charges.

If you suspect you have a less-than-stellar credit rating but aren't sure how bad it truly is, get a copy before you talk financing. It may not be as ugly as you think. And don't simply take the dealer's word that no one will give you a better rate. Shop around for a better deal. You may find a more forgiving lender elsewhere.

Options

Options mean a lot more than mere gravy to your car's meatloaf. Options represent big profits to both the dealer and manufacturer, often fattening a car's profit margin by one-third or more. If you've negotiated a good deal on your car, options offer your dealer a second chance to sweeten his bottom line. With some models offering options at markups sometimes approaching 800 percent (nope, that's not a misprint), you need to work overtime keeping those impulse decisions in check.

We're not advocating driving a "stripper," the industry's term for no-frills, no-fun basic transportation. Besides the fact that you'll curse us every morning as you drive to work listening to AM radio, strippers can be tough to unload come resale time. But when choosing your options, you should consider not only what you like in a car but what the next owner will as well:

Do's: Automatic transmission, air conditioning, and more powerful engines are the guaranteed crowd-pleasers. Try and unload a car without a/c in the dog days of August and you'll see exactly what we mean. Similarly, no one wants to navigate urban traffic with one arm permanently attached to the stick, so if you live in a heavily congested area, stay with automatic. (Sports cars are the one exception to this rule.)

Don'ts: What options should you avoid like the plague? Well, you may love your sunroof, but you can bet the buyer for your car won't give a damn. And in all but the most luxurious of cars, you'll never get back what you paid for leather interiors. Also, just because you're too lazy to reach over to the stereo and change the station, don't assume everybody else will get giddy by the steering-wheel mounted control buttons.

Be wary of worthless options such as fabric protection and paint sealant. A $7 can of Scotchgard and a coat of wax will do the job just as well. (Even if you don't wax, your paint job should hold up pretty well. Car paints have improved, so fading is much less of a problem today.) Also be careful about overpaying for options at the dealership that you can get cheaper elsewhere. Pinstriping and so-called "gold packages" (when chrome just isn't enough!) can usually be done by an aftermarket shop for a fraction of the price.

Finally, we have the last word on extended warranties: no. Your new car will come with a generous standard warranty already, probably the industry standard of three years or 36,000 miles. The extended warranty doesn't activate until the end of the regular warranty, but you start paying for it with your very first car payment.

And because of the high deductibles, extended warranties are really only good for the biggest mechanical disasters. An extended warranty will cost you between $800 to $1,100. To replace your complete drive train would set you back about $700–$800. Are you seeing our point? Sure, you could be the one car owner in 100,000 with the magically self-destructing engine, just as you could be the one person holding the winning Powerball ticket. Frankly, your money would be better spent on the lottery.

When Is the Best Time to Buy?

For such a simple question, there are a lot of different theories, many of them directly opposing. Everyone knows if you want a good price on ski equipment, buy in August. Similarly, I have a friend who loads up on Christmas cards the first week of January. The rules for car buying are far less cut-and-dried, but there are still some that, if you follow them, will put you in a better bargaining position.

Best months: Ask your father when you should buy a new car, and he'll probably tell you that everybody knows dealers are more willing to bargain in January and February when the weather keeps car buyers out of the showrooms. He also might suggest taking advantage of year-end clearances in late fall, when dealers are desperate to clear their showrooms to make room for next year's models.

Both theories sound good on paper, but they don't fully hold up under scrutiny. For one thing, many manufacturers tend to write off the dead of winter and reserve their best incentive and rebate offers when auto buying shifts into high gear. Also, if you are selling your old car, you will be dealing with the same weather-shy, holiday-strapped pool of people as the dealer, so you will have a tougher time getting top dollar. ("Seasonal cars" such as convertibles and 4×4s, however, are best bought off-season, when demand is down.)

Buying in August and September may save you money up front, but by doing so you accelerate depreciation. Here's why: When determining resale value, the model year counts far more than mileage or actual time the car has been on the road. Since most model years end in September, the car you bought in September turns one year old in October, and everyone knows that nobody wants last year's model. Unless you intend to drive the car for years, the early depreciation will usually wipe out any savings. Bottom line: You'll probably save more by buying during a sale than obsessing about the month you buy.

Best week: So while the month may not make all that much difference when buying a car, it does when choosing the right week. Think of manufacturers as very demanding parents who encourage their dealership offspring to compete for parental favors. Each month dealerships must meet certain quotas on their cars if they want access to the manufacturer's hottest models. What this means to you is that if you stumble in at the end of the month ready to buy a Civic and the dealer hasn't met his numbers, he may be very inclined to cut you a deal just to stay in Honda's good graces. Also, dealers often offer cash bonuses to the top-selling employee of each month, so in a tight race your salesperson might be more eager to cut you a deal.

Best day: Shop on the slow days—generally, Tuesday, Wednesday, and Thursday. Not only will you be the center of attention, but you also increase your odds of getting a less-seasoned (read: less-shrewd) salesperson. Many dealerships reserve their big guns for the busy days, so by visiting on the off days you can be reasonably certain your salesperson doesn't negotiate hostage releases on his days off. Avoid weekends in particular when everyone and his brother hits the showrooms.

Best hour: Believe it or not, even the time of day can affect the price you ultimately pay for your car. The last thing a salesperson wants to see is your back as you turn to walk out the door. If he had a dollar for every customer who promised to come back the next day and didn't, he wouldn't be selling cars. If closing time is fast approaching, the salesperson might be more inclined to offer you a good price to close the deal.

USED CARS

There's never been a better time to drive a used car. Besides the obvious cost benefits, such as lower insurance rates, cars are lasting longer than ever. The average car on the road today is over eight years old. A decade ago that number was six and a half. That means if you buy a three-year-old car, you are still getting it at a relatively young age. J.D. Power and Associates even claims that a well-maintained two- to four-year-old car will last longer and have fewer mechanical problems than a new car from ten years ago. Best of all, while new car prices have climbed, used car prices have actually come down a bit.

Leasing has also tilted the auto landscape to the used-car buyer's favor. What do you think happens to the millions of cars that come off-lease each year? Dealers have to move 'em, and because of the heavy penalties for excessive mileage and wear and tear, as a group lessees tend to make for careful drivers. The lessee has already absorbed the car's heaviest depreciation years, doing you a kindness few strangers would.

Still, while it may be easier than ever to avoid the used car crap-shoot of the past, that doesn't mean you can't still get burned. Many of the guidelines for buying a new car apply to used cars as well. Used-car salespeople may not be the polyester-clad, gold-chain-wearing shysters of the past, but you're still not dealing with the pope. Check with your local Better Business Bureau and get recommendations from people you trust.

Consumer Reports and *Consumers Digest* publish annual sur-veys of the most reliable used cars (they are both available on-line as well). *Consumer Reports* presents its results in convenient charts, while *Consumers Digest* tends toward the descriptive. Both evaluate not only models but specific years as well. We find both magazines useful. We like the detailed descriptions of the cars fa-vored by *Consumers Digest* but found *Consumer Reports* a bit more comprehensive: not only does it cover more cars, but it also isn't shy about telling you which cars to avoid.

Next visit www.edmunds.com, the Web site of the Edmund's car guides. Besides safety and reliability ratings, the site provides average retail prices for any used car. It also has a cool feature that adjusts the price for factors such as mileage and equipment.

For example, on a 1995 Toyota Camry, Edmund's deducts eight cents for every mile over 40,100 and adds eight cents for every mile under 36,100. If you will only consider a Camry with a CD changer, Edmund's tells you to expect to pay another $330. It is im-portant to remember, however, that these are national averages. Prices will vary slightly depending on where you live. Still, the site provides you with a good ballpark figure before you go shopping.

Where to Buy Your Used Car

The price you pay for your used car will generally be in direct inverse to the risk you're willing to take. Below, we look at the four most popular used-car outlets and weigh the pros and cons of each.

New-car dealerships: The safest way to buy a good used car. This is the only place you can buy a "certified" car—basically a guarantee that the car has been checked over from top to bottom and meets manufacturer standards. However, peace of mind has a price. Expect to pay an average of $500 to $1,500 more for cars bought here.

Superstore chains: With their acres of used cars, chances are if one of these stores doesn't have what you want, it doesn't exist. A relatively new concept, chains like CarMax and AutoNation USA have already become a permanent part of the suburban landscape. Customers use a computer terminal to identify potential cars. Warranties generally cover one to three months. Selection, a non-commissioned sales team, and reasonable peace of mind are the upsides. However, "no haggle" pricing means you are unlikely to walk away with a steal.

Used-car dealers: To compete with the big guys, independents offer lower prices than the competition. Buying from an honest dealer can save you hundreds of dollars off the same car bought from a superstore. Unfortunately, since assessing the dealer's reputability can be difficult, the risk factor rises exponentially. We recommend buying only from an independent dealer you've heard good things about and who is willing to let you have the car checked by an outside mechanic.

Private sales: For the truly thrifty and adventurous, getting a car through the classifieds is the only way to go. If you would rather eat dirt than pay for a dealer's overhead, break out the classifieds. Since these cars are almost always sold "as is," they carry the greatest risk. But if you're careful, buying a car this way can save you big bucks. Just be sure to perform the tests in our used car checklist and always have a good mechanic inspect it before you negotiate with the seller. That way if the car needs repairs, you can try to deduct it from the price.

LISTEN UP! No-brainer Savings Advice

Just because you're in the market for a used car, don't forget that many of the money-saving rules that apply to new cars work just as well for used. For example, buying that '95 4×4 in August will cost you less than buying it in slushy December. Incentives and rebates don't just benefit new-car buyers; during the sales period, the reduced prices tend to lower the resale value of their used siblings as well. For a listing of current rebate offerings, check out www.edmunds.com.

Beyond Kicking the Tires: The Used-Car Checklist

You should have a mechanic check out any used car you're serious about buying. But at $60 to $100 a pop, that can get expensive fast. By putting the car through these quick do-it-yourself tests, you'll limit the number of trips to the garage. We rank the list in descending order of importance. If the car fails any of the top examinations, get out while you can. You can probably let slide one or two red marks near the bottom. Obviously, you should also consider its price when deciding if the car is worth it. An $800 junker you plan to use strictly as a way to get back and forth from the train station will naturally have more problems than the $5,000 sedan your grandmother wants to unload.

___ Listen closely to the engine. A noisy engine could indicate damage from overheating.

___ Make sure the transmission is in good condition by shifting gears. It should shift smoothly. A "mushy" or grinding shift may indicate trouble down the road.

___ A green slime around the radiator means a bad radiator. Don't let anyone tell you that it's normal. (When is green slime ever a good thing?)

___ Check for rust on the doors, inside the trunk, and around the wheel wells. A little rust on a very old car may be unavoidable, but late-model cars should be rust-free.

___ Mismatched paint on body panels may indicate the car has been in an accident. Don't automatically disqualify a car for this, but be wary. Be more forgiving of older cars. If the car is fairly new, however, the owner may be trying to unload a repaired car that never fully recovered.

___ Check under the car for leaks. Again, if it's an older car, cut it some slack. A small leak can usually be repaired cheaply.

___ On a safe street, slam on the brakes hard. Good brakes shouldn't vibrate, screech, or pull to the side.

___ With the engine idling at operating temperature, check the dipstick. A burned smell or a darkish color may mean a major transmission problem, or it could simply mean the transmission is overdue for a servicing. Have a mechanic check it out.

___ If the car has suspiciously low mileage, check the seats and pedals. Excessive wear may mean a tampered odometer.

___ When you turn on the ignition, the "check engine" light should come on briefly. If it doesn't, the owner may have removed the bulb to conceal engine trouble.

LISTEN UP! No-brainer Savings Advice

Now you can hire a private investigator for your used car. Just give Carfax (www.carfax.com) the vehicle identification number (or VIN, kind of like a social security number for cars) for your car, and Carfax will provide you with a complete history of the car. If the car now has 40,000 miles on its odometer and Carfax tells you that the car had 70,000 miles on it the last time it changed hands, you know something stinks in Denmark. Carfax claims to find a red flag in one in nine cars, which makes the $12.50 charge well worth it.

A Word on Trade-ins

Ah, convenience. In these accelerated times, who doesn't love it? 7-Elevens, ATMs, fast food . . . these days the superharried can even buy their salads pretossed at the supermarket. Of course, we pay a premium for it, but we justify it as a cost of twenty-first-century living. So when a dealer offers to take your old car off your hands as he slides you the key to your new one, should you consider it? Placing a classified ad can be a real headache. Nobody wants to spend how many Saturday afternoons waiting for God-knows-who to show up at your door. You've got a ready buyer standing right in front of you.

Without exception, you will *always* get less for your car in a trade-in than by selling it yourself. At best, the dealer will offer you the wholesale value of the car. He has to factor in repair work and operating costs along with any warranty he might offer with the car. You, as a private seller, can get a figure closer to retail. Trading in can also tip the scales in the dealer's favor when it comes to negotiating, because it gives him two figures to manipulate, the price of the new car as well as the value of the trade-in. You run the risk of getting confused and flustered by all the numbers being thrown your way.

Selling your car privately doesn't have to be traumatic. In our own highly informal survey of people who've sold their cars through the classified ads, it usually takes about four or five appointments and a collective total of about five hours to unload their car. Not a bad deal considering that those five hours netted them hundreds of dollars more than if they had gone the trade-in route. Being honest and upfront about the condition of the car will make the experience substantially more pleasant and less time-consuming. After all, the prospective buyer is going to see the car anyway, so you're just wasting everybody's time if you describe your car as a "cream puff" and neglect to mention that the passenger door is missing. People tend to notice these things.

LEASING FOR DUMMIES

Hands down, leasing is the worst way to pay for the car you drive. We'll say it again louder: *leasing is the worst way to pay for the car you drive.* Ask any sucker why he leases his car, and he'll inevitably say, "I get a new car every couple of years." With a small downpayment, lower monthly payments, and the satisfaction of always driving a late-model car, leasing seems like a "can't lose" proposition. Unfortunately, the realities of leasing paint a very different financial picture. With the average price of a new car costing more than a year at Harvard, it's easy to understand why one in three new cars are leased today. Some auto industry analysts predict that in the next few years more people will lease than buy. And the joke is, most of these people can't afford the car they're in. Remember that next time you're driving to work in your Toyota and it seems like you're the only person on the planet not behind the wheel of a $60,000 German engineering marvel.

Leasing is really just a fancy word for long-term renting. You never actually own the car. You pay for the use of the car over a designated period, usually two or three years, and then return it to the dealer. You make monthly payments to the dealer, which cover both the substantial depreciation to the car and an interest rate that is often higher than those available at a bank. At the end of the contract, you have the option of purchasing the car.

Leasing may raise your standard of living, but it's an illusory boost: you are driving a car that in the normal world you could never afford. That sets a dangerous precedent. As we all know, once you get used to a certain level of comfort, giving it up becomes almost impossible. (Anyone who's ever had to take a pay cut will understand.) When your leasing contract is up, you will likely find yourself tempted to maintain appearances by leasing a similarly unaffordable car.

Leasing also encourages irresponsible budgeting, because you never, ever have to save money for your dream car. Simply walk into the dealership, sign some papers, and you're on the road with a car you did nothing to earn.

"Hold on," you say. "Since I would be paying for the depreciation anyway if I had bought the car outright, leasing doesn't seem like such a bad idea. It gives me the opportunity to try out the car for a couple of years, and if I'm not happy with it, I can just return it. I won't get stuck with a car I hate." That's a nice theory, but dealerships are not charities. When you factor in your lease payments plus the purchase price at the end of the lease, should you decide to keep the car, you will almost always pay more than had you just bought the car new.

Then there is the problem of leasing lingo. Before you can figure exactly what you're getting yourself into, you need to understand terms like "capitalization cost reduction," "residual value," and "money rate." Leasing contracts are notoriously (and many would argue, intentionally) complex, and if you're not good at deciphering legalese, you may run into all sorts of nasty surprises after you sign on the dotted line.

In the early nineties, the Florida attorney general's office launched an investigation into leasing practices and discovered an industry rife with fraud and misrepresentation. In its report, the office identified thirty common ways dealers defraud leasing customers, ranging from failing to credit a trade-in (essentially taking the car for no money) to concealing the true interest rate. Today, federal regulations have cleared the air somewhat, but leasing still has a long way to go. In one recent survey, at the end of their contract leasors were asked to evaluate their leasing experience. Over one third said they would never lease again.

Your leasing agreement will also come with enough stipulations and restrictions to drive you bananas. When Brad and Paula leased a new SUV, they could barely make the monthly payment, but in SUV-crazy Los Angeles, they desperately wanted an upgrade from their last car. Their first shock came hours after they signed the papers. They applied for insurance and discovered that the leasing agreement required them to buy a much more comprehensive (and therefore expensive) policy. Of course, this was stipulated in the fine print of the contract, and if they had 20/10 vision and squinted, they might've even been able to read it.

Surprise #2 came when the couple drove to New Orleans on a

cross-country road trip. Every leased car comes with an annual mileage allowance, usually between 12,000 and 15,000 miles. Go over that limit and you start paying by the mile. In effect, your car becomes a taxicab, and you a trapped passenger. Brad and Paula learned the hard way that 12,000 may sound like a big number, but when it comes to miles, it's pretty skimpy.

They burned through 4,000 miles to New Orleans and back, leaving them with just 8,500 to get them through the next eleven months. "It's a nightmare," Paula says. "I drive forty minutes to work each day and spend most of the commute sweating as the numbers of the odometer roll upward. Plus, now I have to worry about fighting with the dealer over the definition of 'normal' wear and tear. Do you think sweet-and-sour sauce on the carpet constitutes 'normal'?"

With everything we've pointed out, it should be obvious leasing is the wrong way to go. If you still won't take our word for it, how about a higher authority's? Here's what Robert Eaton, the former chairman of Chrysler, said about leasing: "I believe the best thing to do is purchase the vehicle outright. Truth in leasing is upon us, and I think once all the facts are out on leasing, people will realize it's not a good thing." He probably knows what he's talking about, don't you think?

INTERNET CAR SHOPPING

Imagine a world with no car salesmen. A world devoid of sleazy pressure tactics, pushy sales pitches, and cheap polyester suits. A world where, from the privacy and comfort of your own home, you could point-and-click for a new or used car and know that you were getting the perfect car at the absolute guaranteed lowest price. Guess what? It doesn't exist.

At least not yet, anyway. As E-commerce changes the way America spends its Benjamins, it was only a matter of time before the auto industry got wired. Buying a new or used car over the Web can potentially save you a lot of time and money, but it carries no guarantee that it will automatically deliver the best deal.

SUV: Silly Unnecessary Vanity

If it's a small world after all, why is everything around us getting so damn big? Whether you're supersizing it at McDonald's, slurping down a forty-ounce Coke at the local megaplex, or burning it all off by doing laps around a Super K, it seems the nineties have been about one thing: size really does matter.

Cars have been no exception to the "huging" of America. Where once every college graduate craved a cute little two-seater ragtop to zip off into the real world, now she wants a yacht-on-wheels, better known as an SUV. Detroit couldn't give these things away twenty years ago; now they sell over 1.5 million a year. Maybe people think that driving something called an Explorer or a Navigator will put them in touch with their inner cowboy, but the truth is for most people these things are about as necessary in the real world as the Pony Express.

Now I know what you're going to say. You feel safer in an SUV. You like the cocoonlike security SUVs provide if you're involved in an accident. But here's the rub: What are you protecting yourself against? A Toyota Corolla? The pedestrian crossing the street?

No, you're really protecting yourself against other SUV drivers, who probably chose their car to protect themselves against you. It's the freeway equivalent of an arms buildup. (That feeling of safety is a somewhat illusory one as well. Because of their higher center of gravity, SUVs are 40 percent more likely to flip in an accident. And, if you get thrown from the car, the longer fall seriously lowers your chance of survival.)

And another thing (can you tell this is a hot-button issue for us?): With their poor mileage per gallon and heavy weight-load, these things are hell on both the environment and your wallet. Many of our nation's older highways simply weren't designed to handle that much extra weight. Engineers predict that the Brooklyn Bridge would suffer serious structural damage if too many SUVs were to drive over it at the same time. Insurers love them because they can sock their drivers with higher rates.

So do yourself, other drivers, and the environment a favor—when it comes to car buying, keep it sane. Remember that today's status symbol is tomorrow's embarrassment. If you don't believe us, just ask your parents what they did with their old waterbed.

Many on-line car shoppers assume that the cost advantage of the Web—lower overhead, less advertising, fewer personnel—automatically translates to lower car prices. That blind faith can cause you to spend a lot more money for a car than had you endured the bad coffee and haggling at a dealership. We suggest using the Internet as an additional resource, but not your only one.

Below we explain how the different sites can help you surf and save. One warning: Web sites change faster than Madonna's accent, so by the time you're reading this your experience might be substantially different from ours. Don't blame us, we didn't invent the Internet. Al Gore did.

Just the Facts

edmunds.com, kbb.com, and consumersdigest.com: Make one of these sites your first stop before you prepare to cyber-haggle. All three provide the very important dealer invoice price as well as the manufacturer's suggested retail price for the car you want. In addition, kbb.com, the Web site for the Kelley Blue Book, tells you the all-important holdback rate, which is the additional discount the manufacturer gives the dealer beyond the invoice price. This will give you a better idea of how much room the dealer has to negotiate. If you know what you can spend but aren't sure what you want, check out consumersdigest.com's clever search engine. It will list cars in your price range and even tabulate the cost of additional features.

Auto enthusiast magazines: Most major auto magazines have Web sites that offer the same car reviews and car "face-offs" found in their pages. Just keep in mind that they often soft-pedal their evaluations to avoid pissing off their advertisers.

Manufacturers' Web Sites

These sites offer a good starting point for customers in the "just looking" phase. At the minimum, each site provides basic information on models, programs, and services, as well as a directory of authorized dealers. Prospective car buyers are spared a Saturday afternoon collecting brochures from every dealership in town. The more sophisticated sites even allow you to plug in the features you want and spit out the MSRP (manufacturer's suggested retail price) for your options-loaded dream car. At the time of writing, only GM and Chrysler have begun actually selling cars over the Internet (and only in a few states), but that is likely to change. Show-off Toyota treats its Web visitors to a 360-degree tour of their favorite cars.

Dealers in Cyberspace

Autobytel.com, carpoint.msn.com, carsdirect.com: These sites work essentially the same way. You plug in the car you want, and the site submits your request to an affiliated dealer in your local area. Within twenty-four hours that dealer is supposed to contact you with a competitive quote. Of course, there is no guarantee that another local dealership won't beat that price, although theoretically the dealer should pass some of his sales and marketing savings to you. Some of the car sites deal in used cars as well.

Keep in mind that the dealer is ultimately far more important than the site that steered you there, and no individual site has a lock on the dealers offering the lowest prices. Your best bet is to submit purchase requests to several sites to ensure you're getting the best on-line deal.

CAR MAINTENANCE MADE SIMPLE

You don't have to be a grease monkey to keep your car running smoothly. Drivers waste millions of dollars every year on car repairs that could be avoided with an ounce of preventative medicine. The tips below are simple enough for anyone to follow, even those who don't know their radiator from their alternator and think a trannie is just another word for RuPaul.

1. Keep a close eye on your gauges—oil pressure, voltage, and, most important, temperature. At the first sign of overheating, pull the car over and get a tow. An overheated engine can destroy the two most expensive parts of a car, the engine and the transmission. Running an overheating engine for even just a few minutes can do hefty long-term damage. Racing home to avoid the tow charge is probably a losing gamble.

2. Change your oil every 3,000 miles. Although many manufacturers say cars can go as long as 5,000 miles between oil changes, your engine will stay cleaner and run better with more frequent oil changes. Your car will thank you with fewer repairs and a higher resale value. Quality counts, too. Stick to the name brands like Valvoline and Quaker State.

3. Check your oil and transmission fluid levels. Initially, oil level should be checked every 1,000 miles and transmission fluid every six months, but after you've driven your car awhile, you will know if they need to be checked at more or less regular intervals. It takes about a minute to check each and it'll keep unnecessary repairs to a minimum. You may want to check power steering and brake fluids as well, although it's less important because your car will give you a warning before heavy damage occurs.

4. Accelerating hard on cold days will cause excessive wear on the transmission and engine. While you no longer have

to wait for a car to warm up in winter, accelerate gradually until the car has been running awhile.

5. Keep tires inflated to proper levels. (Look on the front door jam placard for recommended tire inflation.) Over- and underinflation compromises safety and wears tires out more quickly. A set of new tires will set you back between $260 and $360. A tire gauge that fits in the glove compartment costs about $4. As a bonus, you'll also boost your mileage per gallon a bit.

6. Just like your own body, your car needs regular checkups to stay fit. Many newer cars can go up to 100,000 miles without one, but older cars need more frequent attention. Follow the manufacturer's recommendations for tune-ups.

7. Keep your hinges lubricated. If your door squeaks when you open it, you are grinding the hinges. A sagging door will affect the resale value of your car or force you to make a repair that could be avoided with a $2 bottle of lubricant.

8. Wash and wax. Washing your car regularly keeps dirt away from moving parts and preserves your paint job. Waxing once a year in normal weather conditions will go a long way toward fending off rust. Don't pay for these services—you can do just as good a job in your driveway as the car wash can.

9. Treat your car like a patient. Your car will usually tell you when it isn't feeling well. Get to know your car's normal behavior so you'll know when it's acting up. Clunks, grinds, rattles—no amount of wishful thinking will make these problems go away, and ignoring them will inevitably make them worse. Take care of them quickly and you'll be less likely to find yourself caught with your hood up and your engine down.

Source: Little World of Cars, Rocky Point, N.Y.

RENTAL CARS

When does $40 \times 7 = 368? When you're standing at the car rental counter trying to figure out how that Ford Taurus you rented at $40 a day ballooned into something considerably more budget-busting. You ask the agent behind the desk to decipher the charges to you. In response she looks at you as if you're one of God's less-gifted creatures. She sighs, and points to the seventeen clauses you initialed on the contract. "Gee," you say to yourself, "that collision-damage waiver seemed like a good idea at the time." Is this what they mean by "new math"?

No doubt about it, the rules and policies concerning rental cars could bewilder even Einstein. Between rental-car contracts, state laws, credit card policies, and your own insurance, it's easy to see why so many of us would rather pay the additional fees than risk making a mistake that could leave us on the line for thousands of dollars. However, with a small amount of planning ahead and a couple of phone calls, you can leave the counter without feeling as if the rental agency just took you for another ride. Before you reserve, try the following:

- *Book early.* Most rental car chains, like airlines and hotels, rely on computers to track customer demand and manipulate prices accordingly. Booking early guarantees you a reservation, but, unlike a restricted airplane ticket, it doesn't lock in the price. So if you call a few times after and are offered a better rate, you can cancel the reservation and rebook.

- *Ask for a corporate rate.* Many agencies offer discounted rates to employees of major corporations. While usually no more than 10 percent, it's still an easy way to lower your bill. This is where you begin to appreciate the true beauty of centralized reservations systems. You don't even have to work for one of the big corporations. Hell, you don't even have to work. I called to make a reservation once and asked if they had a special rate for Sony employees. I was told no, and undeterred, I claimed to also do freelance work for Viacom. (A forgivable lie.) Did they have a rate for that company? Yes, it turns out, they did, and I got the rate. Don't worry about getting caught. The folks at the rental agency have better things to do.

- *Hunt for good deals.* The travel section of your newspaper is often chock-full of ads offering special promotions and discounts. Look for special offers tucked in with your credit card or frequent-flier statements. If you can sift through the junky solicitations and magazine offers for *Troutfishing Monthly*, you'll often find vouchers for discounts or free upgrades. Also, if it doesn't matter what day of the week you travel, avoid Wednesdays, which is the busiest and therefore usually most expensive day to rent, and go on the weekend, when rates are often discounted by as much as 50 percent.

- *Fuel up before you drop off.* Before you whisk off in your borrowed wheels, you will often be offered the option of prepurchasing gas. Don't do it. The price per gallon will be more than you will pay at any gas station. Give yourself an extra ten minutes before dropping off the car to refuel. Never return the car without filling up. Prices are often double those at the pump. The only time you should ignore this rule is if you're on business and billing the whole thing to your stingy, ungrateful boss. In that case, drive around the lot in circles until you're running on fumes.

- *Don't forget the Web.* Most people know of sites that offer discounted airfare, but few know that the rental fleets have gotten in on the act. Priceline.com recently added rental cars to its menu, and most of the major agencies now offer great last-minute rates on their company Web sites. Like the airlines, availability varies greatly by area and demand, so it's probably not a good idea to bank on this method if you absolutely must rent a car. Have a reservation as a backup. If the Web beats the rate you were quoted, then you can simply cancel the existing reservation. One more caveat: Don't assume that the Web "bargain" quote is the absolute rock-bottom. Technology may be wonderful, but it can be inconsistent. Sometimes the national reservations number will still quote you a better rate. Check both.

Should I Pay for the Collision or Loss Damage Waiver if I Already Have Car Insurance?

The short answer is probably not. Yes, it can be scary walking away from the rental counter personally on the line for a $15,000 car, but there's a fairly good chance you're already covered by your own auto policy. Most policies extend to rentals as well. A phone call to your agent will clear things up. You will most likely be responsible for the deductible, as well as for any loss of income the rental company will incur as the car is being repaired. And if you total a rental worth more than your own car, your insurance will probably only cover you for the value of your own car. (That should make that Lexus rental far less tempting.) Also, most insurance policies only cover rentals in the U.S. and Canada, so driving an underinsured car on the Autobahn is probably not the brightest move.

If you're a decent driver with a good policy, your financial exposure is small enough that it's probably not worth the additional money. (Or, if you're lucky enough to rent in New York or Illinois, you're spared these choices entirely. Renters are only responsible for a small deductible, provided they don't rent the car for a game of highway chicken.) If, on the other hand, you drive like Mr. Magoo after he's had a few too many, consider springing for the additional coverage. Alternately, use a credit card that offers secondary insurance, which picks up the expenses your policy doesn't.

But If I Don't Own a Car and I Don't Have Insurance, My Credit Card Will Cover Me, Right?

Again, you will *probably* be fine with the protection your card offers, but you should always double-check with customer service beforehand. Credit cards revise their policies regularly, and if you missed the notice stuffed into your last statement, that's your problem. As a general rule of thumb, Amex cards of any color provide insurance, as do most gold Visa and Mastercards. Classic cards are hit or miss, and some Optima cards exclude coverage. Most cards cover the U.S. and Canada and beyond, but again, you'll only know for sure if you call and ask.

CHEAT SHEET

If you're just starting out, your car may be your biggest expense. Americans tend to forget that a car is first and foremost a means of transportation and not a pricey status symbol. As a result, we waste a lot of money trying to win the parking lot wars.

- *Consider buying used.* Depreciation is the biggest expense drivers face. When you buy a well-maintained used car, the previous owner has already taken the biggest depreciation hit.
- *If you do buy new, shop around for a competitive loan.* Higher interest rates and long repayment plans can add thousands of dollars to the cost of your car. Try a credit union and a few banks before you hear what the dealer has to offer.
- *Where you buy a car can make a big difference in your budget.* Check the Internet, the classifieds, and the superstores before you commit. Used-car dealers often offer better prices than the franchises, but stick to one who comes recommended.
- *Do not lease.* Only fools lease. Period.

9

What If I Get Hit
by a Bus?
Insurance 101

W ho wouldn't fault you for feeling invincible? You're in your robust twenties, well beyond chicken pox and decades before the bones start creaking. Short of getting hit by a bus, nothing can hurt you. Hmmm. . . . Last we checked, bus homicides were hardly an epidemic. However, the minor to major catastrophes that can happen in life are more than enough reason to stay insured. In a world where bad things happen to good people, not having insurance may compound the misfortune by making it a financial tragedy as well. Having enough insurance ensures you won't get hit with a devastating financial surprise.

For the strapped, those monthly premiums you stuff into the envelope each month can be a tempting place to start slashing the bills. Chances are you won't get into a serious accident while driving to work, you won't come home to find your house in flames, and you won't slip on a banana peel and break a leg. Most of us would never notice we're walking around without enough insurance. You could be reasonably certain life would continue on or close to schedule, freeing you up to worry about more important things like why the guy you met at the dog run hasn't called yet.

But what if something bad did happen to you? Those surgeon's fees, repair bills, and legal judgments add up fast. You could face a lifetime of debt just by trying to save a little money on your premiums. We know someone in her early twenties who lost everything she owned when her apartment caught fire. She wasn't insured. Every piece of furniture, every appliance, every article of clothing—up in smoke. Think about all those times driving back from the mall wondering if you could really afford the new $100 Nikes you had just bought. Now imagine what squeezing a whole new life on your Amex would do to your finances.

We're not trying to keep you up at night. All we want to do is point out that when it comes to insurance and your financial health, cheaper is not always the way to go. Unlike most of the other chapters in this book, the emphasis here is not on spending less. Rather, the goal here is to help you find the *right* amount of insurance at the *best* price for your personal situation (while saving money along the way!).

Car Insurance: Don't Leave Home Without It

What Does 100/300/50 Mean, Again?

It's been a long time since driver's ed. If you've been on the road for a few years, you know insurance is legally required—but who remembers exactly what each term covers? Let's review the five basic types of coverage you can carry:

Bodily injury and property damage liability insurance: This is the part of your insurance that lets you off the hook if you're at fault in an accident. Liability insurance covers the other person or people injured in the accident, your passengers, and any property you may damage (other cars, fences, cows, etc.). One crude way to remember this is to think of liability insurance as covering everything around you *except* your body and your car. Most states require liability insurance, although minimum levels vary by state. Don't confuse the minimum with the recommended amount. Most state minimums barely cover a broken leg and a couple of

X rays. After that, the injured party can come after you to recover his expenses.

Liability insurance is broken down into a standardized shorthand of three successive numbers. The first two refer to bodily injury and the last number to property. For example, if you carry 100/300/50, your insurer will pay up to $100,000 for one person's injuries, but no more than $300,000 total for all injuries if more than one person is injured. Your company will also pay up to $50,000 in property damages. Liability is usually the most expensive part of your premium.

Collision and comprehensive coverage: If you've ever been involved in an accident, you know that your heart drops not once, but twice: once after you hear the sickening crunch, the next time when the mechanic hands you the bill. Cars may be getting more reliable on the inside, but as car designs use larger and larger panels, they get more expensive to fix. In a recent safety test, the Insurance Institute for Highway Safety crashed various makes of cars and trucks into different kinds of barriers. After four crashes at a top speed of 5 MPH, vehicles sustained up to $7,498 in body damage. And that's going 5 miles per hour! Do you know anyone who drives that slow?

Collision covers the cost of damage to your car regardless of fault, but it comes at a price. Besides the deductible, premiums can be high, and insurance companies are notorious for undervaluing your car if it gets totaled. Comprehensive protects your car from natural disasters, freak accidents, and the LAPD (just kidding). Though no state requires collision and comprehensive, if you borrowed money to buy your car or if you lease, you will likely be required to carry both as part of your loan agreement.

Uninsured or underinsured motorist coverage: Just because you obey the law and carry auto insurance, you can't assume every other driver is following your law-abiding lead. The Insurance Information Institute says that 13 percent of all accidents are either caused by uninsured or hit-and-run drivers. Have an unfortunate run-in with one of these people and you may be facing large medical bills and no way to collect.

Sure, you could take the slob to court, but who do you think drives around without insurance? No one in the Fortune 500, I assure you. You'll be suing a 17-year-old burger-flipper or someone celebrating his first day off parole, and you'll be left holding an award the defendant can never hope to pay. You'll never see a dime of the money owed to you. You learned a long time ago that sometimes being right just isn't enough. This is one of those times.

Medical Payments Insurance: As the name implies, this insurance covers your medical bills for injuries sustained in a car accident, regardless of fault. It also covers your passengers. Any health insurance plan worth having will cover you behind the wheel, so for most people this type of coverage is unnecessary. People living in a "no-fault state" may be required to carry a minimum of medical payments insurance, however.

Three Ways Not to Get Screwed by Auto Insurance Companies

1. *Check your credit.* Before you shop around for the best rate or take a defensive driving class, the first thing you should do before choosing an auto insurer is check your credit report. In the loopy logic of many insurance companies, a sloppy credit history can make you a higher risk than your Camaro-driving neighbor with five moving violations under his belt.

   What does your credit report have to do with your driving ability? Evidently, quite a bit. Insurance companies are increasingly using credit reports as a way to predict your behavior and responsibility. A careful and regular payer, they reason, is more likely to look both ways before crossing an intersection. To us, these seem like dangerous generalizations only slightly less fair than punishing you for your age or where you live, but there's nothing you can do about it.

Over 300 insurers now consider your credit report when setting rates, and they aren't likely to change anytime soon. We've heard of cases of drivers paying almost double because of their spotty credit history.

We suggest getting a copy of your report from one of the credit bureaus before you begin your insurance search. If you're already on the road and insured, check your report anyway. If there's a mistake on your report, that might be the reason you're paying through the nose for insurance even though you've never seen the inside of a traffic court. (See page 200 for contact information for the major credit bureaus.) Conversely, if you have a good report, there's a good chance you're being rewarded with lower insurance rates. Even if you don't, as time clears up your blemished report, you can look forward to better rates in the future.

2. *Shop around.* The difference between what each insurance company charges for the same coverage can be truly astonishing. Call five different agents and you will most likely be quoted five different rates. Consumer surveys routinely turn up cases of insurers offering the same policies at rates sometimes 400 percent higher than their competitors. I tested this recently and called three different companies for their rates. For *identical* policies, Geico quoted me a rate of $1,179, Progressive quoted me $1,429, and State Farm tried to soak me for $1,768. The lesson: Don't assume all insurance is created equal.

Of course, no one expects you to spend a month slogging through the phone book to get the absolute rock-bottom insurance rates. (In fact, signing up with a third-rate insurer to save $75 will probably cost you more grief in the long run.) We suggest narrowing your search to six insurers that sell their policies through different avenues. Choose two that use agents, two that sell direct, and two on the Internet (see box, page 182). That should give you enough variety to be confident you're getting a good deal. Talk to a couple insured friends about their experiences with the customer service lines as well. If you have an A+ driving record, be sure to call Amica (800-992-6422), a picky insurance company that keeps its premiums low by insuring only good drivers. If you already have insurance, ask your current carrier if you qualify for a better "pricing tier." If your driving record or credit report has improved since the last renewal period, you may be eligible for a lower quote, but you have to ask for it.

3. *Raise your deductible.* When you buy insurance, your premium (a fancy word for "bill") is determined by the amount of coverage and the deductible. The more coverage you carry, the higher your premiums will be. Conversely, the lower your deductible, the lower your premiums.

The first rule of insurance: Gamble on the deductible, not on the amount of coverage you carry. Here's why: The majority of people pay far more in insurance premiums than they ever get back. We carry insurance in case we are in the small minority of unlucky people who actually need it. (Insurance has got to be one of the only things we buy and hope to never have to use.) You may never, ever file a claim, but you will always pay a premium.

Why pay years of higher premiums for the off-chance that you *might* have to use your deductible? If you have a serious accident, you will be far more concerned that you have enough insurance than whether or not you're on the line for the first $200 or $800. High deductibles are annoying; too little coverage can be devastating.

Of course, there are exceptions. If you drive like a pimply teenager, then carry collision with a low deductible (and stay out of my neighborhood!). But for the vast majority of people in their robust, healthy twenties who view driving as transportation and not bloodsport, the higher deductible is the way to go.

That's All Great, but How Do I Figure Out How Much Car Insurance I Need?

We wish we could just serve up twenty or so questions to design a tailor-made insurance policy for you. Unfortunately, what works for *Cosmo* magazine doesn't hold up for car insurance. The truly important factors to consider can't be easily quantified. To my mind, the number of moving violations you accrue in a year is a less accurate measure of your driving ability than how confident you feel behind the wheel year-round. Likewise, if you've never had an accident, but regularly drive home Saturday nights praying your blood-alcohol level isn't over the legal limit, you're not exactly a low-risk driver.

Besides your driving habits, you should also consider your net worth when choosing a policy. Although a judge can levy a judgment against future earnings, she is likely to take into account your present finances when determining damages. The less you have, the less she will likely order you to pay. (Unless you were doing something phenomenally reckless or stupid when you caused the accident. In that case, you can kiss any judicial sympathy good-bye.)

Actual time spent on the road is naturally a factor as well. I'm a pretty good driver, but I wouldn't feel too comfortable crisscrossing the country with 25/50/25, my state's minimum required insurance. Finally, consider the traffic conditions and the area you live in. Statistics show a direct relationship between population density and number of claims filed.

Thirteen Surefire Ways to Cheaper Auto Insurance

- *Drive more safely.* Duh, right? In its obviousness, this has gotta rank up there with "buy low, sell high," but driving defensively is still the single best way to reduce your rates over the long term. The fewer points on your license, the more brownie points you score with your insurance company. Two moving violations in a year will usually knock you into a higher, more expensive risk category for the next three years. An accident you caused definitely will.

Make a conscious effort to change your bad driving habits: don't try to beat the light, don't roll through stop signs, and don't interpret the speed limit in cat years. You may get away with it the first ninety-nine times, but inevitably there'll be a cop around the corner just waiting to spoil your streak.

- *Don't drive an SUV.* Yep, here we go again. Liability premiums for SUV owners may soon go through the (already-elevated) roof. An influential study recently released by the Insurance Institute of Highway Safety found that liability claims for drivers of the largest SUVs were on average a full 40 percent higher than claims for drivers of standard passenger cars.

  Even more disturbing, the same study found that passengers in subcompact cars are forty-seven times more likely to die in a collision with an SUV than the occupants in the larger vehicle. Hardly a surprise, since many SUVs look like they could swallow a Toyota whole. In response, some insurers have begun charging premiums 5 to 20 percent higher for SUV owners, with other companies likely to follow suit in the future.

- *Take a defensive driving class.* Most insurers give you a break on your rate if you take a defensive driving course. The class will cost you money, and it's hardly a festive way to spend a Saturday, but it's worth it—you can shave up to 10 percent on your rate for the next three years. Your insurer can provide a list of local certified classes.

- *Call your agent on your birthday.* The Jewish religion considers children to be adults once they reach their thirteenth birthday. Auto insurers don't. They consider twenty-five for single women and thirty for single men to be the delineating birthdays between childhood recklessness and adult responsibility. (Married men reach adulthood at twenty-five; mar-

ried women become adults on their wedding day.) Most insurance companies will offer you lower rates when you reach
these birthdays, but it is your responsibility to make sure
they don't forget.

- *Drive less.* Insurers rightfully figure that the less time spent
  on the road, the fewer opportunities to have an accident.
  They reward low-mileage drivers with lower rates. Mileage
  limits vary by insurer, but generally range from 5,000 to
  7,000 miles a year. If you can keep your mileage within that
  range, sign up with an insurer who offers low-mileage rates.
  (By the way, don't think you can hide that cross-country road
  trip from your insurer. She may ask for documentation of
  your mileage.)

- *Fight traffic tickets.* The actual costs of a summons go way
  beyond the fine. Rack up too many points on your license,
  and hello, assigned risk. In the earlier chapters you learned
  to put a dollar figure on the consequences of your actions.
  Traffic tickets are no exception. Considering that one serious
  moving violation infraction can set you back hundreds of
  dollars in increased premiums, you should request a hearing
  for any ticket that you feel was issued unfairly. And considering how helpful and efficient DMV offices are, it's not surprising that many people would just rather mail the check
  than deal. But you know better. It's well worth the hour or
  two investment to overturn the ticket. Dress neatly, be polite,
  and bring any witness statements or photographs to the trial.
  I've had a couple of tickets dismissed this way and kept my
  insurance at a reasonable level.

- *But if you do lose, pay them quickly!* The DMV hates
  scofflaws and, depending on the infraction, they may suspend
  your license if you fail to pay your tickets. Insurance companies, however, love scofflaws because they can use the suspension as an excuse to raise your premiums. Case in point:
  After my license was suspended for not fixing a broken
  headlight, my insurance company jacked up my annual premium by $300 for three consecutive years. They used that

suspension, even for something as minor as a broken headlight, to move me into a higher risk category.

- *Buy direct.* Sales-related expenses such as salaries and commissions gobble up about 25 percent of a traditional insurance company's revenues. For companies that cut out the intermediary and sell policies directly over the telephone, that figure is closer to 15 percent. If you're persistent, you should find a company that passes some of the savings on to you. Two of the biggest direct sellers are Geico Direct (800-841-3000) and Progressive (800-AUTO-PRO), although they may not be available in all states.

- *Drive a car thieves don't want.* You have a Lojack and a club; your grandfather has a 1993 Monte Carlo. Guess who has the better theft deterrent? When thieves go shopping, they look for cars they can unload quickly for resale or a chop shop, not necessarily the most expensive cars. Find out which cars in your area are more likely to be stolen, and don't buy one. The Insurance Institute for Highway Safety (1005 N. Glebe Rd., Arlington, VA 22201) keeps an updated list of high-risk cars. Write to them and ask for the Highway Loss Data Chart, or visit their Web site at www.hwysafety.org.

- *Drive a cheap car to repair.* When it comes to auto maintenance, don't assume "parts is parts." An alloy wheel for a 1997 BMW 325i costs $779; the same part for a 1997 Toyota Camry costs $332. Quick-to-fix cars naturally cost less in labor than those that require a Ph.D. to get under the hood. Insurance companies keep sophisticated statistics ranking the models in order of cost to fix. Expensive repairs = higher premiums. Ask your insurer or mechanic to recommend a make that won't cost a fortune to repair.

- *Drop collision on older cars.* The average U.S. driver is in a car accident once every seven years. That includes everything from the smallest fender bender to the accordion smashup. If you carry collision, you're paying seven years' worth of collision premiums for that one unlucky day you should have taken the bus. That makes sense if you're protecting a $35,000 Range Rover, but not if your car has been around the depreciation block a few times. For older cars, the odds are on the insurance company's side that you'll pay more in collision premiums before you ever put in a claim.

- *Be honest, just not completely honest.* Anyone who's shopped around for auto insurance knows what it's like to get the third degree. How many miles from work to your house? Date of your last moving violation? How long have you lived at your current residence? Have you ever been financially insolvent? How long have you been at your current job? And so on . . . While you may wonder what some of these questions have to do with your driving ability, every answer moves your rate slightly higher or lower. You should be truthful, not just because it's the right thing to do, but because the insurance company verifies the information you give them and will adjust your rate when they catch your whopper.

  However, if you think something might slip under the radar, sins of omission are okay. For example, why mention that out-of-state speeding ticket you got? There's a decent chance it won't show up on your agent's computer. You can also round up your time at your current residence, which is used to determine your stability and is hard to verify.

- *Ask about these common discounts:*

  - Nonsmoker
  - No accidents in three years
  - Antitheft devices
  - Antilock brakes
  - Good grades for students
  - Automatic seatbelts
  - No cell phone in car
  - Airbags

LISTEN UP! No-brainer Savings Advice

If spending countless hours on the phone calling insurance agents leaves you feeling dazed and confused, the Web offers a partial remedy. Modeled after sites such as Travelocity.com and Priceline.com, which deliver the lowest prices on things as diverse as airline tickets and groceries, there are now a number of life and auto insurance sites that take care of the comparison shopping for you. Although the prices they quote should never be considered the last word, as a starting point for a great life or car insurance rate, it's worth the surf.

- Progressive (www.auto-insurance.com) asks for information about your driving history and then provides you with their quotes as well as rates from other insurers. While the site is easy to navigate, when I tried to compare a basic 100/300/50 Progressive policy to State Farm's, I could only get a State Farm quote that also included collision. Naturally, the State Farm rate was higher. Another caveat: Competitors' rates may also not be the most up-to-date.
- Geico (www.geico.com), 20thCentury (www.20thcentins.com), and Nationwide Direct (www.ndirect.com) don't compare their rates to the competition, but they do offer you the convenience of getting a quote without having to spend twenty minutes on the phone.

If you need life insurance, try Instantquote (www.instantquote.com), quickquote (www.quickquote.com), or insuremarket (www.insuremarket.com). All will mine their databases to find the lowest-priced level-term policies based on the information you provide. But take the results with a grain of salt—some of the sites, like insuremarket, have a limited number of companies in their databases while others don't ask enough questions about your medical history to provide a truly accurate quote.

As of this writing, the other types of insurance still have a ways to go before providing truly helpful sites, so for the time being you'll still have to shop the old-fashioned way for health, disability, and homeowner's insurance. But even if you do use the Web to shop for insurance, it's always smart to check with a few agents to ensure that you're getting the best deal.

Filing a Claim

You can win the premium battle and lose the insurance war if you file a claim and don't get all the money owed to you. Don't just assume that choosing a name-brand company will protect you from a lowball settlement. Some of the biggest insurance companies regularly top the lists of policyholder complaint lists.

Claims typically account for 75 percent of an insurance company's expenses. In recent years almost every major insurer has aggressively struggled to knock that percentage down. Short-changing valid claims is one of the unfortunate ways many companies try.

Remember the Fifth Debtly Sin: *Though Shalt Not Waste.* What do you call not fighting for money you're entitled to? When you pay a premium, you are "buying" a commitment from your insurer to live up to its end of the bargain. Accepting less than you deserve because it's easier than fighting is as wasteful as dropping a $20 bill and not picking it up because you're too lazy.

If you suspect your insurance company is dragging its feet or stonewalling you on a claim, you may be right. Insurance companies understand human nature and know you're eager for the check. They know many people will meekly accept a lowball offer rather than face an impenetrable and intimidating bureaucracy. Here are some tips to help you get treated fairly in your hour of need:

- *Report a claim quickly and accurately.* Make sure you save all receipts related to your claim and other crucial paperwork such as the police report and witness statements. You should also look over the police report to ensure that it is accurate.

Jason vs. Goliath

Many years ago my little Honda Civic was demolished when a car blew through a red light and broadsided me. The Civic was long past its prime but certainly worth more than the $400 the guy's insurance company offered me. The insurance company wouldn't budge (they even had the nerve to imply that their offer was generous!), so I sued and won $1,200. Not a bad take for an evening's work.

- *Keep a record of all phone calls and letters.* Log not only the time and date of your call, but whom you spoke to and the content of the conversation. Send any correspondence certified and ask your insurer to put in writing how they came to their settlement decision. Once it's in writing, they can't change the reason if you can disprove their findings. You can also challenge the insurance company's methods for arriving at that figure.

  For example, some insurers use consultants to check ads and used-car lot prices to determine the value of your car instead of relying on the Blue Book. That may sound fine in theory, but remember who's paying them. You wouldn't trust Pat Buchanan to count the ballots in an election. Don't count on a consultant's objectivity.

- *Threaten to complain to your state's insurance commission.* Insurance companies hate interference from regulators. Though they can't force your insurer to pay, with a little luck your insurance company may raise their offer just to keep the commission out of it.

- *Know the statute of limitations.* In many states, you lose the right to sue an insurer a year after you've filed a claim. Ask your agent what your state law allows.

- *If all else fails, take 'em to (small claims) court.* This is your option of last resort. Chances are you will not get enough out of a verdict to justify your legal expenses. However, there's nothing preventing you from paying $5 at your local court-house to drag your multibillion dollar insurance Goliath to court.

RENTERS INSURANCE

Right now, most of you are probably saying, "Renters insurance? Why do I need that? I thought the goal here is to save money, not spend more." And it is. But for a couple hundred bucks a year, renters insurance protects you from the burden of replacing your possessions if something unforeseeable should happen. It also comes with personal liability protection, which protects you not only if someone is injured in your dwelling, but if you accidentally injure someone off-property as well. An acquaintance of mine was walking her dog when a man tripped over her dog and fell on the sidewalk. The jerk sued her and won almost $100,000. Her renters insurance picked up the entire tab. It was the best $250 she ever spent.

Next time you have a quiet evening at home, take a look around you. Make a mental tally of your stuff. This includes furniture, appliances, your CD collection, and the suit you wore once to your brother's wedding. It adds up quickly. Chances are you have a lot more than you think. (That at least should make you less depressed when you wonder what you have to show for all those bills.) I did this recently and was surprised to discover that the cost of replacing everything I owned easily surpassed my debtload at its absolute worst. If something ever happened to my apartment, how would I possibly come up with the cash to replace a decade of acquisitions?

If you already have car insurance, you may be able to save 5 to 10 percent by taking out a renters policy with the same carrier. Ask about discounts as well; many carriers will give you a reduced rate if you have deadbolt locks, a smoke detector, or a house full of nonsmokers. You should also take a look at Insuremarket.com and

Insweb.com. Both sites will help you comparison ship for competitive rates, although the transaction must be finalized off-line.

It's hard enough for most of us to make ends meet without the devastation of an unforeseen catastrophe. Yes, chances are your apartment will never be visited by a flood or fire, but acts of God aren't exempt from Murphy's Law. I have four friends who have lost possessions from apartment damage.

My former co-worker Raquel came home from work one day to find her collection of vintage dresses soaking wet from a burst pipe. Raquel, already shouldering $80,000 in grad school loans, estimated the dresses' value at $4,000. Although she wasn't covered, at least she hadn't lost her sense of humor. "Just don't invite me to any cocktail parties in the future," she said after the flood.

LISTEN UP! No-brainer Savings Advice

Make sure you're covered for the *replacement cost* of your property. When you sign up for renters insurance, your insurer will offer you two types of coverage. The *replacement cost* covers the cost of replacing the item new, while the *actual cash value* essentially gives you the amount you would get for the item if you sold it at a garage sale. Avoid the sting of depreciation and opt for the replacement cost policy. It costs a bit more, but it's better than having the insurance company insult you with a check for $300 for all your worldly possessions.

THE BODY IS YOUR TEMPLE: HEALTH INSURANCE

Unless you've been living under a rock for the last decade, you know we're facing a crisis in health care. What is a God-given right in other Western countries is a partisan tug-of-war in the U.S. of A. The statistics are downright disturbing: even in these flush times, 55 million people in this country go without health insur-

ance. And the trend is only getting worse. With each 1 percent increase in premiums, another 200,000 people drop their coverage.

It may be tempting to skip health insurance in your twenties.
After all, when will you ever feel this healthy and invulnerable
again? If you're in debt, the temptation to skip this considerable
expense might be very appealing. Don't do it. Even if you're an
Olympic contender who eats nothing but steamed chicken and
broccoli, you are risking *permanent financial ruin* should something unforeseeable happen. The one time you forget to look both
ways before crossing the street, you land on someone else's hood.
Or your neighbor's pit bull decides you smell just like a Beefy
Burger. Once, between jobs, I went without health insurance for a
month and promptly dislocated my shoulder snowboarding. It set
me back $500. Bottom line: shit happens.

If your employer offers you health coverage, you're good to go.
Chances are you have to pick up part of the premium yourself, but
it's most likely a fraction of the cost if you had to carry your own
policy. But if you have to insure yourself, you should take the time
to familiarize yourself with what's out there. The biggest way to
save money on insurance is to choose a plan that doesn't over- or
underinsure you. Too much coverage will cost you money in
higher premiums. Too little may hit you with a heap of unreimbursed medical bills you are responsible for.

The Two Big Choices

In a perfect world, you would be able to walk into any doctor's office, flash your insurance card, and walk out with your wallet intact.
Yeah, sure. And monkeys might fly out of . . . well, you know the ex-
pression. The truth is, over the last ten years, health care choices have
become increasingly restricted as health care costs have skyrocketed.
While there is no such thing as the perfect plan, you have a choice of
two different kinds of insurance, fee-for-service and managed care.
Each has its advantages and disadvantages.

If money were no object, *fee-for-service* is the way to go. You can
go to any doctor you want, change at any time, and visit a specialist

when necessary. This freedom will cost you, however. Premiums are typically expensive, and there is always a deductible you must meet before your insurance kicks in. Your insurer usually picks up 80 percent of the bill, leaving you with the remaining 20 percent.

But since we know money is an object, *managed care* is probably the better option. There are two kinds of managed care programs, HMOs (health maintenance organizations) and PPOs (preferred-provider organizations). You've probably heard at least a couple HMO horror stories, and speaking from experience, I can tell you many of them are true.

When my college employer switched from a solid health plan to an HMO, I am not exaggerating when I say I got my first taste of third world medicine. First, I had to wait hours in a dirty waiting room to see a harried, nameless doctor who would then decide if my condition merited a specialist. Not every HMO will be that grim, of course, but they have a dicey reputation for a reason. If an HMO is your only option, then of course go with an HMO rather than remaining uninsured. Just remember that the quality of the plans can vary widely, even for plans with comparable premiums. Make sure you talk to some friends about their experiences and read the fine print before you sign up.

Preferred provider organizations offer a comfortable compromise between the two. With a PPO, you get to choose from a wide selection of doctors within their network. The premiums are usually substantially lower than fee-for-service, and with no deductibles and minimal copayments, you don't have to worry about a nasty surprise waiting for you at the nurse's counter.

Self-Insurance Made Simple

Yes, covering your insurance bills yourself can be an expensive proposition. If you choose to go it alone or your current employment situation doesn't provide coverage, use this table to help you find the best policy. The major carriers, such as Blue Cross/Blue Shield or Aetna, are good places to start, but call at least four insurers to guarantee a competitive rate.

If you are . . .	Between jobs (short-term)	Unemployed	Self-employed and loving it	Flat broke
Perfect world	A short-term policy that runs from two to six months. It is renewable once. Offered by most major carriers	See if you can stay on your previous employer's plan through COBRA, which allows you to pick up your employer's insurance for 2 percent more than the current premium	A comprehensive plan (fee-for-service, PPO) that covers hospital stays, check-ups, and lab tests	Catastrophic coverage
Plan B	Catastrophic insurance (aka the "what if I get hit by a bus?" plan). Covers hospital stays and related charges	Interim insurance, or, at the very least, catastrophic	Try an HMO or join a trade association and sign up for their group coverage	See if you qualify for Medicaid. If not, now is the time to test your parents' generosity

LISTEN UP! No-brainer Savings Advice

Ever wonder why it takes more paperwork to get reimbursed for a simple checkup visit than it does to adopt a baby from Romania? Well, now you can delegate your headaches to a third party, who will get down and dirty with the insurance company and do their best to wrest your money from the tentacles of the insurance company.

Known as claims assistance professionals, these intermediaries are trained to navigate the labyrinthine path to reimbursement. If you feel you're being stiffed by your carrier, you might consider hiring a CAP to plead your case. Most charge

$20 to $80 an hour, so unless the amount you're entitled to exceeds $1,000, you might end up with higher CAP fees than the original disputed amount. The Alliance of Claims Assistance Professionals (630-588-1260) can refer you to a CAP in your area. Since most states don't require a license to practice, you should request one who has worked in the insurance or medical field.

DISABILITY INSURANCE

It's hard enough making ends meet on your salary now, right? But what if you had to cover the same expenses without a weekly paycheck?

Unthinkable, right? Disability insurance gives you a fighting chance to remain independent should you become physically or mentally unable to work.

Most people in their twenties don't give disability insurance a second thought. They either confuse it with worker's comp (which only protects you on the job, not off, like disability) or put it near the bottom of their insurance priorities. But for most people in this group, disability insurance is actually much more important than life insurance. It is much more likely that a person will become disabled than face an early appointment with the grim reaper.

Most other types of insurance become more valuable as you get older—you need more coverage to protect your increasing assets (hopefully) and increased medical expenses (unfortunately). But if you're young, in good health, and still living paycheck to paycheck, your most important assets are the money-earning decades ahead of you.

Think about it. You wouldn't buy a $200,000 house without homeowner's insurance. Now take a minute and subtract your age from sixty-five, the legal retirement age. Multiply your current salary by the number of work years ahead of you. Without even considering future raises, that's a huge number. Now you see what you're protecting and why disability insurance is so crucial.

Chances are your employer offers at least some type of disability plan, but don't take it for granted that it offers sufficient coverage. If your company plan covers 60 percent of your income with no cap on the length of time you can collect, you're probably okay, but many plans limit the payout amount or the months you can collect. You don't want to jeopardize your recovery by rushing back to work because you're out of money.

If your current plan is inadequate or if you're self-employed, you should strongly consider purchasing additional disability insurance. However, this very necessary insurance can be expensive. Here are some tips to keep in mind when shopping for a policy:

- *Avoid the daredevil surcharge.* Professional wrestlers and skydiving enthusiasts naturally pay higher premiums than a book editor with a weekend chess addiction. If you already have a high-risk job there's not much you can do about your premium, but if you plan to switch to a higher risk profession or take up a dangerous hobby in the near future, buy a policy a few months before you do. And while you're at it . . .

- *Sign up for disability insurance* before *getting professional help.* Mental and nervous conditions account for the second highest number of disability claims. Fairly or not, you may get hit with higher rates if you are seeing a therapist.

- *Make sure you buy a noncancelable, guaranteed renewable policy.* That's a mouthful, but it's important. If you file a lot of claims, this prevents the insurance company from canceling your policy or raising your premiums to prohibitive levels.

- *Take advantage of a flexible benefit plan.* Many employers allow their employees to tailor their benefits package to their own needs. If you're lucky enough to work for a company that offers this, consider increasing your disability benefits and taking less coverage somewhere else.

- *Shop around.* We're beginning to sound like a broken record, but quotes can fluctuate wildly from company to company. Call Termquote (800-444-8376), which will send you a list detailing several disability policies. However, they can only quote you rates from companies in their database. You should also check with a few insurance agents and compare their rates with direct-sellers such as USAA Life Insurance Company (800-531-8000).

- *Increase your elimination period.* This is the period you must wait before you begin to receive benefits. By increasing the number of months of the elimination period, you can often substantially reduce your premium.

Send In the MIB

Top secret codes, no government regulation, and a nefarious-sounding name. Is the MIB something out of a George Orwell novel? No. The MIB refers to the Medical Information Bureau, a major organization that operates under a blanket of secrecy straight out of *1984*. As an organization that disseminates billions of pieces of individual medical history each year to insurance companies, the Medical Information Bureau wields an inordinate amount of influence. And chances are you've never even heard of it.

When you apply for health, life, or disability insurance, the MIB is the central database that insurance companies use to examine your medical history and lifestyle. The MIB keeps files on only a fraction of the population, but you won't know if they have anything on you unless you write to them. Not only will your 1995 bout with hepatitis be in their files, but it will also note your bungee-jumping obsession. Insurers can use this and other information to deny you insurance or charge you much higher premiums.

Think of it as a credit report for your health. And like a credit report, you should correct errors on the report that may lead to unjustifiably higher premiums. To get a copy of your MIB report, download an application at www.mib.com or write the MIB at P.O. Box 105, Essex Station, Boston, MA 02112. You can also call them at 617-426-3660.

- *Be wary of exclusions and conditions.* Many insurance policies will include provisions making you ineligible for benefits if you are injured or get sick in certain ways. Preexisting
medical conditions or dangerous hobbies are two of the more
common exclusions. But there is no *right* or *wrong* way to
become disabled.

   Being unable to work, however temporary, is frightening
enough without having to worry if your particular disability
qualifies for benefits. Look for a policy with as few exclusions as possible. The definition of disability will vary from
policy to policy. If you are a professional, make sure you are
covered for *own occupation*, which will cover you if you
cannot do your specific job. This is better than an *any occupation* policy, which only provides benefits if you can't work
at all. Also shoot for *residual benefits*, which will pay you a
percentage of your benefits if you are disabled but can still
work part-time.

LIFE INSURANCE: WHO NEEDS IT?

If you're single and dependent-free, you don't need life insurance. Period. If you're married, childless, and both of you have
thriving careers, you don't need life insurance either. We'd bet
most of the people reading this book fall into one of these two
categories.

Life insurance protects people who rely on your income if you
die. It is not some morbid consolation prize—"Well, Patty's dead,
but she left me a $50,000 death benefit. Paaarrtyy!" Rather, it
gives your dependents a financial cushion to go on without you.

However, if you are the primary breadwinner in a young family,
you need life insurance. How much and what kind you need will
vary depending on your situation, but for most young families
term insurance is the way to go. Term insurance covers you for a
specified number of years. At the end of the term, you have the option of renewing the policy or dropping it (although many insurers

require a physical before renewing). Termquote (800-444-8376)
and Quotesmith (800-556-9393) are two companies that provide
rate information for a large number of term policies. Don't let any-
body talk you into buying a *permanent life insurance* policy. The
perceived advantages are pretty much all BS. Whatever advantages permanent life offers can almost always be found somewhere else for less.

Stupid Insurance

You now know that there is no one-size-fits-all policy when it
comes to creating an insurance program right for you. In assem-
bling the right insurance package for your needs, you need to
consider everything from where you live to your number of dependents to how much you have in the bank. Car insurance, health insurance, disability, renters insurance—the list of policies you
shouldn't live without is indeed a long one. I don't know about
you, but that strikes me as enough insurance for one lifetime. Concentrate on being smart about the insurance that really matters and
skip the worthless mountain of junk out there. Among the biggest
money wasters:

- *Flight insurance.* You've probably heard the statistics that
  say a person has a better chance of getting hit by lightning
  than going down in a plane, yet each year many of us still
  feel compelled to plunk down extra cash at the airport for
  this useless insurance. Maybe you got stuck in turbulence
  one too many times or maybe you just believe God rewards
  the extra-cautious, but flight insurance is never a good idea.
  If you don't have dependents, you don't need flight insurance. Period. If you're worried about dependents, look into
  life insurance. If you're still not convinced that flight insurance is a waste, find a credit card company that offers it for
  tickets charged to their card.
- *Extended warranties.* With increasing competition and strides
  in technology, today's manufactured products are made bet-

ter and last longer than that crummy record player you got as
a kid. If you are concerned that the product won't last, you're
better off paying more for a better quality substitute. The
premium you pay for the warranty will often cost more than
having the item fixed at a repair shop. And once you consider
that many extended warranties only cover the parts of the
product least likely to break, their value becomes even more
questionable.

- *Insurance for small appliances.* These premiums generally
  represent such a high percentage of the cost of the item that
  it's just silly to buy them. When a friend of ours went to an
  electronics chain store to buy a new $45 Walkman recently,
  she was offered a "guaranteed replacement for one year"
  policy for $20. And while yes, she could conceivably drop
  the Walkman in the street as her bus is pulling up, chances
  are she won't.

  Cellular service providers are notorious culprits in this
  game. For $3.25 and a $35 deductible, Sprint offers insurance for cell phones bought directly from them. Sound like a
  good deal? Consider that the policy only covers manufactur-
  ing defects, so if you lose it or drop it (they swear they can
  tell if you did), you're on your own. Use insurance to protect
  yourself against catastrophe and disasters, not life's daily
  annoyances.

- *Credit card insurance.* As you know by now, you should be
  highly suspicious of anything offered by the plastic people.
  For a "small" monthly fee, many credit card companies offer
  a whole host of "protections" that are either unnecessary,
  overpriced, or outright misleading. You may think that your
  issuer is offering you a great deal for protection against
  lost or stolen cards, but guess what? Federal law already re-
  stricts your liability to no more than $50 per card, so you
  won't be ruined if your card falls into crooked hands. Likewise, ignore solicitations that offer to make your payments
  should you become unemployed. These plans only cover the
  minimum monthly payments until you get another job, not

your outstanding balances. The pricey premiums tacked onto your card each month almost never justify such a measly benefit.

- *Alien abduction insurance.* If E.T. wants to take you home for show-and-tell, you will probably have bigger things to worry about than loss of income. Yet a London-based insurance brokerage has clearly tapped into postmillennial madness and sold 20,000 alien abduction policies (mostly to the "feeble-minded," admits an executive at the firm). Before you scoff, the company actually made good on one claim and shelled out about $1.5 million to a guy who claims to have been whisked away for forty minutes in a UFO. (We know you weren't actually considering this, but we thought it was just too bizarre not to mention.)

CHEAT SHEET

Going through life un- or underinsured is penny-wise and pound-foolish. As a twentysomething, you've got years ahead of you to lead a rich, fulfilling life. Insurance protects your future from a tragedy that can permanently destroy your financial freedom.

- *Check your credit report before you get car insurance.* Insurers assume financially responsible people make better drivers. If there's a mistake on your report, you may be hit with higher premiums.
- *Take advantage of insurance discounts.* Auto insurers offer a wide range of discounts for everything from driving an ugly car to turning thirty. Ask your insurer for a list of available discounts.
- *Bad things happen to renters, too.* Don't skip renters insurance. For a couple hundred bucks a year, you can protect both your belongings from disaster and yourself from litigious visitors.

- *A box of Band-Aids is not a health plan.* You cannot go without health insurance, plain and simple. If you are self-employed or not working, the chart on page 189 can help you find the right plan for you.
- *The squeaky wheel gets the cash.* If you think your insurance company is shortchanging you, speak up. Persistence and meticulous record keeping can help you resolve your claim to your satisfaction.

10

Now What?

Welcome to the next day of the rest of your (debt-free) life.

Think of everything you've accomplished. You don't cringe when you open your credit card bill each month. You've stopped hemorrhaging money on crap you don't need. You're making better choices about banking, insurance, and car payments. You're living within your means and loving it.

Now here's one simple bit of advice: *Don't blow it!*

Achieving financial solvency and having control of your monetary destiny is a new experience for most of us. We're so used to rationalizing our bad habits and justifying our poor choices. We live in a culture of debt—car payments, student loans, mortgages, and credit cards—that being in the hole seems almost natural.

MISTAKES, YOU'VE HAD A FEW—NOW STOP DOING IT YOUR WAY AND DO IT OUR WAY

Your commitment to debt-free living doesn't stop at a zero debt balance. You've got to resist the temptation to start the unhealthy cycle of debt again. Unfortunately, a lot of people rescue themselves from the financial abyss only to fall back into their old habits after a few retail binges. A zero balance on your credit card means you have that much money to spend: zero.

Confessions of a Debt Junkie

Brian is a 28-year-old publicist with a casual demeanor and attitude that belies his tragic addiction to debt. His sob story is pretty typical. "After I graduated from college, I had almost $3,000 in credit card debt, student loans, *and* a car payment. I thought I was hopeless." The first few postgraduate years were tough. His job paid less than $30,000 and he could only make the minimum payment on his monthly credit card bill.

After a couple of years (and a couple more thousand dollars charged on his Mastercard), Brian landed a promotion and a significant raise. "I was tired of throwing away money for rent and servicing my high-interest debt. I knew if I was ever going to buy a house I needed to get serious about my financial situation." So instead of converting his pay increase into a new car or a fancy vacation, he started committing his extra money to his credit card debts and student loans.

"I remember the day I mailed in my last student loan payment," Brian recalled. "It was like I'd just been given my life back." Unfortunately, he also felt like he was empowered to spend, spend, spend! "I saw that zero balance on my credit card statement, and then I looked at the $5,000 credit limit and I thought—'I've got five thousand bucks to spend!' "

To "celebrate" attaining debt-free nirvana, he binged and splurged. He bought almost a thousand dollars' worth of clothes and electronics and took his girlfriend to a pricey resort. "It's like celebrating your graduation from AA with a keg party," he added, chuckling at his own misfortune.

Now he's back back to his no-frills lifestyle, literally "paying" for his mistakes. Again. "I'm not going to make the same mistake this time," he promises. "I don't want to spend the rest of my life eating mac & cheese so I can pay off a stereo I bought three months ago."

It's surprising how often smart, successful, rational people continue to make the same stupid mistakes two, three, and four times. Here are some things you can do to prevent those blunders:

- *Continue to keep track of your spending.* You don't have to save every receipt and agonize over every penny, but you need to have a good monthly estimation of how much money is flying out of your wallet. Making lists of everything you *need* helps keep impulse purchases to a minimum.
- *Pay cash whenever possible.* In a perfect world we'd advise you to cut up your credit cards and pay for everything in cash. Everyone knows this isn't practical. However, it's best to save your credit card for emergencies or when no other form of payment is possible. A debit card that withdraws money directly from your bank account is a great (and nearly universally accepted) alternative.
- *Look at the big picture.* The simplest solution is sometimes the toughest to accept. Think about the money you spend— every time you reach into your wallet. Are you overpaying? Can you afford this? Is there a cheaper alternative? Is this something you really need or want? What's your special purpose in life? If you can answer all of these questions (especially the last one), then you're making a sound purchase rather than a finance-busting impulse buy.

CREDIT REPORTING AGENCIES: THE IRS'S EVIL TWIN

Credit reporting agencies are gigantic, unholy bureaucracies that make lots and lots of mistakes. It's wise to get periodic updates of your credit reports to ensure that the credit agency is dispensing the correct information about your financial shenanigans. The last thing you need when you try to buy a house or a car is a screwed-up credit report because some deadbeat shares your last name. It's also wise to check your report at each company to make sure the information is consistent.

LISTEN UP! No-brainer Savings Advice!

Still having trouble controlling those acquisitive cravings? Channel those urges into something that'll be paying dividends long after the thrill of the impulse buy has worn off. We're talking about the stock market, and with on-line trading firms such as E*trade and Datek, it's easier than ever for the small investor to get started. When you open an account and start investing wisely, you can splurge without guilt. A number of reformed debtors we spoke to claim that investing in stocks this way has helped them stay out of trouble. "I will always be a consumer at heart," says one. "But now I accumulate stocks instead of buying more junk I don't need. I can still take pleasure in owning something, only this time it's something that I won't throw out in a year or two." Just be careful of buying on margin, which gives you the power to trade with money you don't have. If your stocks go down in value, you could find yourself right back in the hole you climbed out of.

The top three credit agencies are Transunion, Experian, and Equifax:

Transunion	Experian	Equifax
P.O. Box 390	P.O. Box 2104	P.O. Box 105873
Springfield, PA 19064	Allen, TX 75013	Atlanta, GA 30348
216-779-7200	800-392-1122	800-685-1111
transunion.com	experian.com	equifax.com

These reports generally cost between $8 and $16 (although in some states the law requires these companies to provide your report for free). You can order by writing a letter, calling, or by filling out an easy on-line form. If you are denied credit because of information on your credit report, you can get a free copy of your report by sending a written request.

"But I didn't charge $147 for *Wizard of Oz* collectible plates!"—What to Do If You Notice Mistakes on Your Credit Report

Unfortunately, mistakes by credit reporting agencies aren't uncommon. Sometimes, credit reporting companies will just screw up and report late payments or defaults for no particular reason (save general incompetence).

Each credit reporting company has a process for disputed items. Generally, you send them a request for an investigation. Don't be nasty, confrontational, or accusatory. Simply explain the situation and provide documentation—like a copy of the bill in question—if any is available. If a mistake is detected you should ask the agency to send a corrected report to anyone who requested a report over the past year.

You've Been a Naughty, Naughty Boy or Girl: Repairing Your Credit Rating

So you really screwed up? You forgot to pay that Amex bill (for the eleventh time). *Repo Man* is a movie based on your life. Sallie Mae is going to bust down your door and take back your diploma. Unfortunately, if you've been delinquent or defaulted on payments, you *will* get red marks on your permanent record.

Don't get too stressed out. Everyone can earn a second chance—even you.

There are some simple, straightforward ways to start repairing your credit if it's a problem. Here's what you'll need to do to clear your good name.

- *Pay your bills on time.* Yep, it's a simple rule that many people can't seem to follow. Creditors notify credit reporting agencies if you're habitually late sending your payment. This

Clair Repair

"They wouldn't even let me get a corporate card. I felt like a complete incompetent!" Clair confided one afternoon over coffee. "At twenty-five I'm starting to pay for my irresponsible early twenties." Clair, a graphic designer, had lots of cash-flow problems early in her career. "I worked freelance and I had to put everything on my credit card—a computer, all my work supplies, whatever. As a freelancer it takes *forever* to get paid, so I got way behind on all my bills. I even defaulted on one card." Obviously, this left quite a smudge on Clair's credit report.

As a girl with a bad (credit) reputation, Clair needed a way to clean up her act. "After I got a full-time job with a decent salary, I started paying all my bills on time or even before they were due. I was dedicated to demonstrating I was a good, trustworthy citizen." Clair also wrote a letter to the credit reporting agencies, asking them to include information about her permanent job. She included a pay stub to verify her salary.

"The added information definitely helped when I rented the apartment. Since the information was already on the credit report, I had less to explain to the landlord." Clair explained. "Now my reputation precedes me."

can screw you up when you try to rent an apartment, apply for a mortgage, or buy a car. Make a habit of paying your bills a couple of days before their due date. This makes you more cognizant of the way you manage your money and also ensures that you won't be counted late because your payment takes an extra day to arrive in the mail.

- *Consider signing up for a Web-based bill-paying service.* If you're the forgetful type, you may consider signing up for on-line banking or a Web-based bill-paying service. These convenient services provide a centralized way to manage your monthly bills and prevent you from having to write a check, search for a stamp, and find a mailbox. On-line banking allows you to manage your account from the bank's Web site or by using special software. This service allows you to pay bills by simply typing in the creditor's address, account number, and the amount you wish to pay. The bank then debits your account and transfers the money directly to your creditor. Web-based bill-paying services work almost the same way. You simply log on and fill out a form with your bank's routing number, your checking account number, and your bill information. Once all of this information is confirmed, the service allows you to electronically transfer money to pay your bills with a minimum of fuss and confusion.

Paymybills.com

This convenient, easy-to-use site is one of our favorites because it means you never have to get another bill in the mail. When you sign up, Paymybills.com starts to receive all of your paper bills. The service scans the paper bills and posts them to a secure bill management center. You're notified via E-mail each time a new bill arrives, and then you pay with just a couple of clicks. These bills are filed so you can access them at any time.

Another great thing about this service? You can schedule regular monthly payments for things like rent or your car loan. This is a good way to avoid late fees. However, you have to be vigilant with your bank balance so an automatic debit won't empty out your account.

While the service costs $8.95 a month, the convenience may be well worth it—especially if you're the type of person who consistently racks up late fees.

- Include positive information in your credit report. Sadly, credit reporting agencies don't get paid to write good stuff about you. When it comes to your credit report, it's your job to spread the word.

You're entitled to add information to your credit report that you feel will help your rating. Legally you are allowed to include a statement of up to 100 words involving any credit dispute. The credit agencies must provide this information to anyone who requests your report. You can use this opportunity to include information about salary increases, current credit card accounts where you have a good record, student loans you paid on schedule, or the settlement of disputed bills.

- *Don't screw up.* The best policy is not to get in trouble in the first place. Negative information stays on your credit report for seven years, and if you've declared bankruptcy this will stick around for ten years. Yep, that's *ten whole years* of being a financial untouchable.

BANKRUPTCY FOR BEGINNERS (WE HOPE YOU DON'T NEED TO READ THIS SECTION!)

So, you *really* blew it. If you're in really dire straits and you're considering personal bankruptcy, then you need more help than this book can provide. When you file bankruptcy, your creditors are no longer legally permitted to bug you. They have to cease and desist until a judge can decide your fate.

Here's the 411 on the different types of bankruptcy and how they will affect your life, future, and finances. Neither type of bankruptcy eliminates student loans or back taxes, so if you're in hock to Uncle Sam you're out of luck.

Chapter 7

If you can convince a judge that you have no way of paying back your debts, then you could qualify for Chapter 7. Basically, this means that all your debt is eliminated. This sounds like a fantasy, right? Wrong. The judge then decides if any of your valuable assets—like a house, jewelry, or a car—can be sold to reimburse your creditors.

Chapter 13

When you file for Chapter 13 bankruptcy, the court arranges a payment plan for your debts. These debts must be paid in full, but the judge may waive interest payments and penalties.

Now What Happens?

Your credit report will get a *big* red mark. Chapter 13 stays on your credit report for seven years, while Chapter 7 will haunt you for *ten* years. It will be much more difficult to find a landlord willing to rent you an apartment, and you probably won't qualify for things like cellular phone service. It's possible for someone who has declared bankruptcy to get a car loan or mortgage, but he or she will probably have to pay higher fees than someone with good credit.

If you feel like this is your only option, then you should speak to an attorney who specializes in personal bankruptcy. Otherwise, it's a much better solution for your credit standing (and self-esteem) to get serious about paying off your debt the old-fashioned way.

CHEAT SHEET

- *Commit yourself to debt-free living.* Don't make the same mistakes twice. Continue to be vigilant about your spending habits and think about everything you buy: Do you need it? Can you afford it? Could you find the same thing cheaper someplace else?
- *Check your credit report.* Make sure the credit reporting agencies are giving out correct information. If your credit rating is in the crapper, do everything you can to correct it.

11

Life After Debt: Using Money to Make Money

It's a formative experience. You withdraw money at the bank, and for the first time in . . . well, ever . . . *you have money left over at the end of the month!*

After you pick your jaw up off the floor, it's time to start thinking about the fun part of money—making more. While this book is not intended to give investing advice, there are a few things that are no-brainers for the young, formerly broke, and upwardly mobile.

LIVING PHAT IN FLORIDA: RETIRING IN STYLE

Ah, the golden years. For a lot of us this means golf, grandkids, and a condo in Florida. However, if you're expecting social security to reward you for a lifetime of toil and hard work, then you probably also believe Demi Moore has the breasts God gave her.

As the baby-boom generation ages and millions more Americans are withdrawing from the fund than are paying into it, the social security fund will be maxed out. Short of a miracle, when it's our turn to retire there will be little, if anything, left. Sucks, huh?

Now's the time to start squirreling away some of your paycheck away for your later years. Don't count on winning the lottery. Don't count on generous children who will love you when you can't remember their names. And definitely don't count on Uncle Sam. This is something you have to take care of yourself, and the sooner the better.

But who has the money to save? You do. Anyone can find an extra ten or twenty bucks to save. It's okay to start small. Plus, once you see how quickly the money adds up, you'll start to feel a sense of real accomplishment. The money you save is the money you pay yourself—for your future, your dreams, and your family. Isn't it time you gave yourself a raise?

What kind of savings plan should I choose? We touched on this before in chapter 7, but it's so important we want to hammer it home again. If you read this book in order, some of the info below will be repetitive. If you skipped around (tsk, tsk), now you have no excuse for getting started on a retirement plan. A tax-favored retirement account is one of the most amazing financial opportunities for someone in his or her twenties. The most common types of plans available are the 401(k) and an IRA.

The concept behind each of these plans is the same. You contribute a percentage of your total income, and the government deducts this amount—up to $2,000 for an IRA and $10,500 for a 401(k)—when determining your taxable income. A Roth IRA works a little differently, but we'll discuss that later.

What does this mean? If you earn $40,000 and put 5 percent ($2,000) into a tax-favored plan, then you'll pay taxes on $38,000. Cool deal!

401(k)

This is the most common type of retirement plan at many companies. You choose a percentage of your salary—usually up to 15 percent, with a maximum of $10,500 per year (although the IRS adjusts this figure annually based on inflation). You generally can't touch the money without a severe penalty until you're 59½. It's the government's way of helping you keep your grubby fingers off your retirement nest egg.

One of the coolest things about 401(k) plans is that many employers match a portion of the amount you contribute. In essence, this means your company is giving you *free money.* You heard right: *free money!* If you're lucky enough to work for a company with a matching 401(k) plan, you should definitely take advantage of it. Many companies have "vesting periods," which is the amount of time you need to stay employed at the company to receive the full benefits. This varies by company, so if you have questions about your particular plan you should ask your benefits coordinator at work.

Laying that golden nest egg

Amy, a 29-year-old editor, describes the moment her 401(k) benefits coordinator told her how much money she'd saved. "I was shocked. I thought someone had made a mistake." She signed up for her 401(k) immediately after she became eligible (at her company, this was after a year of full-time employment). She set aside 5 percent of her salary to be deposited into her account every pay period. "It seemed like a lot at the time, but honestly I never missed it. I'm sure I would've wasted it anyway."

Her employer had a generous matching program—doubling Amy's biweekly contribution. Plus, part of the contribution was invested in the company's stock, which consistently outperformed the market. "I forgot I had even signed up for the program. When the quarterly account statements came, I'd just shove them in my filing cabinet and forget them."

After five years, Amy decided to accept another job. "The benefits coordinator told me I had over $30,000 in my 401(k). Apparently my company's stock split and went up pretty dramatically," she recalls. "It's the best thing I ever did."

IRA

An IRA is a great alternative for people who are freelancers or whose company doesn't offer a 401(k) retirement plan. There are several types of IRAs, but the two most popular retirement accounts are the traditional individual IRA and the Roth IRA. Both basically work the same way, except with a traditional IRA you pay taxes when you withdraw the money at 59½. With a Roth IRA, you make your periodic contribution with posttax income—this means when you withdraw the money at retirement, you've already paid taxes on everything. Ask an investment advisor or find a good financial guide to determine which IRA is best for you.

The Miracle of Compound Interest

Here's the benefit of both of these retirement plans: compound interest. Possibly the most important concept ever to come out of the Economics 101 class you slept through in college.

It sounds like a scam. You don't only earn money on the money you invest, you also earn money on the interest of the money you invest. Confused? It's a really good thing—trust us.

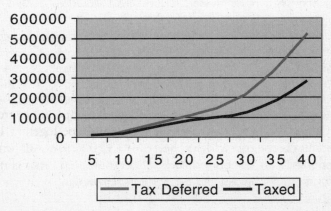

Saving $2,000 a year for forty years

If you invest $2,000 a year in a tax-deferred account like a 401(k) or IRA for forty years starting at age 25 and you earn a modest 8 percent a year, you'll have $518,113 when you retire at 65. A half-million dollars buys you lots of shuffleboard for your golden years.

The most important thing to remember about compound interest? *Time.* How long you keep your money in an interest-bearing account can ultimately be more important than how much you invest.

Saving $2,000 a year for thirty years

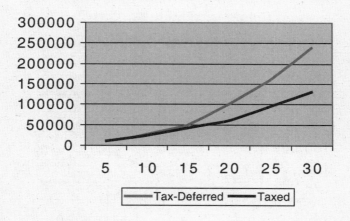

If you started investing $2,000 a year at 35 and earned 8 percent interest, by the time you are 65 you'd have $246,692—that's less than half the money you'd have if you started investing only ten years earlier. This is the incredible effect of compound interest.

Just compare these two charts. If you can scrape together 100 bucks a month at 8 percent interest for forty years in a tax-deferred account, you'll be sitting on a nest egg of $349,101. If you save $500 a month for twenty years in the same account, you'll only have $294,510.

$100 a month for forty years

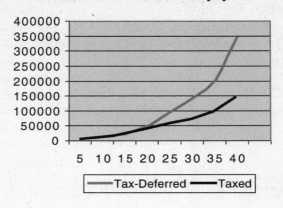

$500 a month for twenty years

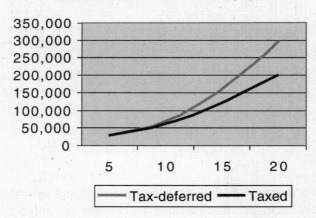

On-line financial calculators are a fun way to motivate good saving habits. You can instantly calculate your future wealth based on variables like percentage of savings to income, rate of expected return, and years until withdrawal. Most financial Web sites and all the well-known portals include links to easy-to-use financial calculators.

INVESTING 101: WELCOME TO THE REST OF YOUR LIFE

Everyone knows the stories. Joe Investor sticks $200 in the IPO of Getrich.com and wakes up a millionaire the next day. Even though most of these stories are complete and utter crap, lots of people feel like they're missing the twenty-first century's version of the gold rush.

It's true—the stock market has been a great place to invest your money over the past few years. But for every story we hear about the instant millionaire, there are lots of regular people investing wisely, earning great returns, and building the kind of savings it takes to buy a house, start a family, or plan for retirement.

Getting Prepared

Before you start any serious investing, it's wise to put a bit of money away in a safe place like a savings account in case you lose your job or have a similar financial crisis. Once you're out of debt, a good rule of thumb is to have enough money saved so you can cover your expenses for two months without any other income. This is a big savings commitment to make, but you'll be glad you did when that rainy day comes.

Money Market Funds

Money market funds are almost as safe as a traditional savings account and typically pay higher interest rates. Many different kinds of companies offer money market funds, including full service banks, brokerage firms, and mutual fund companies. This is a great place to put your rainy-day fund or to save money you know you'll need in the next six to twelve months (maybe you're saving for a down payment on a house).

We recommend setting up an automatic direct withdrawal between your checking account and the company that manages your money market fund. This way a certain amount of cash will be

Fires, Tornados, Psycho Bosses, and Other Natural Catastrophes

Building an easily accessible two- or three-month salary's cash reserve is an essential part of being a grown-up. It prepares you for such disasters as an apartment fire, sudden illness, or getting fired. Joseph, a 29-year-old friend at a Web start-up, used his cash reserve for a personal disaster too many of us can relate to: "Sheila, my boss, was a complete raving lunatic. For me the choice was simple—quit or go completely crazy."

Joseph felt the situation was so unhealthy in his office that he had to quit before he could find another job. "I was desperate. Everyone in the office called her 'Old Yeller,' " Joseph explains, "because she would storm around the office screaming at everyone, even the company's CFO. It was a completely demoralizing, toxic environment." Luckily, Joseph had saved several months' salary in an interest-bearing money market fund. "When I started saving the money I thought I was being a little overcautious. But that money ended up saving my life. It allowed me to take a month off to look for a better job."

Joseph quickly found a happier situation that paid him even better than Sheila had. Whatever happened to "Old Yeller"? Joseph shakes his head. "I don't know. But I found out later she had been fired from her last four jobs in L.A. for the same antics. It's amazing people that destructive can still find work."

transferred into your interest-bearing money market fund once or twice a month—and you don't have to do anything. This is a cool way to force you to save without even thinking about it. After the first month, you won't even notice the money is gone.

Mutual Funds

Mutual funds are a great way for novice investors to get started in the wild world of stocks and bonds. Instead of having to rely on your brother's friend's aunt's cousin who is a stockbroker to pass along a hot tip, you can have a professional manage your money and select the stocks and bonds for you. A mutual fund is a kind of investment that pools the money of lots of people. A fund manager—someone who has spent years analyzing companies and studying the stock and bond markets—invests the entire sum in a selected portfolio of stocks and bonds.

You shouldn't have any unrealistic expectations—remember mutual funds, like individual stocks and bonds, don't always go up. At the same time, historically for long-term investors, equities have been the best place to park your cash. A traditional savings account may not even beat inflation—so you could be actually *losing* money. You know your financial situation better than anyone, so let your conscience be your guide.

Finding the right mutual fund. So if you've made the decision you can tolerate a certain amount of risk, then you need to find the mutual fund that's right for you. There are thousands of kinds of mutual funds. You can select a fund that invests in a particular market sector like technology or energy. You can choose a fund that only invests in big companies or small companies. You can pick a socially conscious fund that only invests in companies that are environmentally friendly or have progressive employment policies. Choosing a mutual fund can be a confusing and bewildering task, but we have some guidelines to help make your selection easier.

Choose a no-load mutual fund. Some mutual fund companies charge a fee called a "load" each time you put money in or take money out of your fund. Honestly, it's kind of a rip-off. There are a lots of quality "no-load" funds that typically outperform their "load" counterparts. There's just no reason to pay the extra money for the same service.

Consider an index fund. Everyone's heard of the Standard & Poor's 500—it's an index that tracks the stocks of the 500 largest companies in the U.S. You can find lots of no-load mutual funds that "track" this index (this means the fund's stock portfolio tries to replicate the performance of the S&P 500 by investing in the same 500 stocks).

Over the past ten years the stock market has been the best place to get an amazing return on your investment. While what goes up must come down, historically—if you're investing for the long term—stocks have been a smart place to start.

Index funds generally have lower management fees because they're not actively managed—that is, the fund manager doesn't choose the stocks. However, many index funds that track the S&P 500 have typically earned returns matching or outperforming most actively managed funds. For the new investor, they're often a smart choice.

Here are some of the most widely known and trusted mutual fund companies:

The Vanguard Group
P.O. Box 2600
Valley Forge, PA 19482-2600
800-871-3879
www.vanguard.com

Fidelity Investments
P.O. Box 193
Boston, MA 02101-0193
800-544-6666
www.fidelity.com

T. Rowe Price
Account Services
Mail Code 17300
4515 Painters Mill Road
Owings Mills, MD 21117-4903
800-225-513
www.troweprice.com

THE FUN PART STARTS NOW: YOU FINALLY GET TO SPEND SOME MONEY

Now the fun begins. Here we start setting long-term goals. These are the things you want to use your savings and wise financial planning to accomplish. Maybe you want to buy a house, get a new car, take some kind of cool vacation, or hire Britney Spears to perform at your thirtieth birthday bash (or maybe not). Now that you're in firm control of your wallet, you can start planning ways to achieve your dreams. Sure, it sounds corny—but it's true.

Here's the last list we're going to ask you to write, and we promise it's going to be the easiest. It might even be fun.

1. List your life goals—everything from the real to the absurd. Some of our suggestions: retire at 50, become a homeowner in three years, take a two-week vacation to Europe, plan a lush wedding, buy a solid-gold garden gnome. Use this opportunity to fantasize.
2. Write down the age you'd like to be when you accomplish these goals.
3. Estimate how much money it will take to achieve these goals.
4. Divide that number by the months remaining until you reach the age by which you want to accomplish your goal. This determines the amount of money you'll need to save every month. Put it in an interest-bearing account like a money market fund.
5. Send us a thank-you note after you've accomplished this goal. (We need constant affirmation!)

Goal	Your desired age when you achieve goal	Amount needed	Monthly savings	Achieved? (Thank-you note sent to Jason & Karl?)
Buy a big screen TV	28	$1,150 (one year)	$95.85	
Down payment on home	33 (six years)	$12,000	$200	

MONEY ISN'T EVERYTHING (STOP LAUGHING)

After pages and pages of obsessing about a single topic, we're going to end this book by offering you a few bits of insight. Money may help you find security and stability, but it won't make you happy. We know you've heard that old line before, but think about it. What are the things that genuinely make you content and cheerful? Spending time with friends? Playing frisbee outside with the dog? Sitting on the couch and watching "The 'E' True Hollywood Story"? Most of the things that make us happy are either cheap or absolutely free.

Unfortunately, this hurly-burly modern world is an environment where omnipresent advertising attempts to make us unhappy with our lives, bodies, appearance, and possessions. *This loaded DVD player shows how cutting edge I am! Using this $40 face cream will transform you into a blinding vision of Madison Avenue* *beauty! These $250 shoes will show everyone at the high school reunion how successful you really are!* It's a bunch of crap—at the same time, it's hard to avoid being influenced by the constant barrage of messages.

Slipping Off the Golden Handcuffs

"I'd become a slave to my possessions," Jeff confided one afternoon. As a successful investment banker, Jeff made more money than almost all of his other friends. "Since I was single, I had no one to spend money on except myself. I bought all sorts of things—an expensive home, a car, thousands of dollars of audio and video equipment." He shook his head, "I surrounded myself with a bunch of expensive stuff I didn't need. The stereo was so complicated, I never figured out how to use it."

He was miserable. In exchange for a huge salary and bonus, Jeff regularly worked twelve hours a day and on weekends. "I never saw my friends anymore. And the more stuff I bought, the more money I needed to pay for it." Finally, he had enough. "I started focusing on saving my money, living more simply, and curbing my insatiable buying habits."

Jeff sold his (almost empty) luxury house, moved into a simple apartment, and started saving more than half of his net income each month. He also set goals: Jeff decided to save his money so he could take a few years off in his early thirties to travel. "It's ironic. I worked and worked to buy lots of things I thought I wanted, and then one day I realized the thing I really wanted was to stop working." He laughed. "Regardless of how much money you make, you can't buy your life back, right?"

Yep, we feel your pain. It's easy to become depressed about the cool clothes, cars, or gizmos you don't have. It's common to feel that your friends who decided to go into higher-paying professions made better choices. The idealism from your teenage and college years ("I'll become a teacher!") seems like a bitter joke when the class idiot (turned lawyer) drives by in his $50,000 BMW.

Sometimes it feels like the whole world is obsessed with consumption—what you buy, what you wear, where you live, and what you drive is somehow synonymous with who you are. Forget it. The day you decide that your personal happiness is not dependent on a bunch of overpriced crap is the day you'll stop stressing out about money. You have something money can't buy: youth and opportunity. Take advantage of both of them.

Quit Your Job (You Heard Us!)

Okay, we know it's not an option for everyone, but for us the real objective to working and making money is to be able to stop working and still make money. Don't think of your job as a place you park yourself until you're 65 and they shove you out the door with a paperweight, office party, and cheap bottle of champagne. Your job is a means to an end—the end being an exciting, fulfilling life where you have an opportunity to explore your interests, cultivate friendships, and build relationships.

This is the real reason for staying debt-free: *Freedom.* Enjoy it. Good luck!

Cheat Sheet

- *Put money in a 401(k) or IRA.* Hey, you're not going to be young forever. Take advantage of tax-favored retirement accounts to make sure your golden years are just that—golden.
- *Invest.* Start educating yourself about mutual funds, money market funds, and other investment opportunities. Make your money work for you for a change!
- *Set goals.* It's simple. Decide what you want out of life and

then go do it. Determine how much money each of your objectives takes, and then start saving aggressively to accomplish these goals.

- *Quit your job. Work to live* rather than *live to work.* Enjoy your youth, life, and freedom.

INDEX